"Wisdom is alwsimply attractive
tions about pray
her book to pray...pray...pray and never stop!"
> **Kathy Collard Miller**
> **Speaker and author of *Why Do I Put So Much Pressure On Myself?***

"The too-busy life of every woman, wife, or mother is what most often gets in the way of an effective prayer life. The very things that mean the most to us--home, family, friends, church or job--are the same ones we allow to keep us from making prayer a vital part of our lives. *When A Woman Prays* teaches you how to move prayer from the role of crisis-management or afterthought to become the central power-house of a full and rewarding life."
> **Sally E. Stuart**
> **Author of the annual *Christian Writers' Market Guide* and a dozen other books**

"...an exceptionally honest book that hits just about every chord a woman experiences in life. But it goes one step further. It teaches women to turn to the only true source that can fill all the empty spaces and offer complete contentment, regardless of what is happening in and around her--God."
> **Alyice Edrich**
> **Freelance writer and author**

When
A
Woman Prays

Tina L. Miller

Obadiah Press

607 N. Cleveland Street	1826 Crossover Road, PMB 108
Merrill, Wisconsin	Fayetteville, Arkansas

When A Woman Prays
Copyright © 2002 by Tina L. Miller

Cover design by Darlene Schacht, Nathaniel Design
Page layout by Tina L. Miller

ISBN: 0-9713266-1-4

Scripture taken from the HOLY BIBLE, NEW INTERNATIONAL VERSION®. (Unless otherwise noted) Copyright © 1973, 1978, 1984 by International Bible Society. Used by permission of Zondervan Publishing House. All rights reserved.

The "NIV" and "New International Version" trademarks are registered in the United States Patent and Trademark Office by International Bible Society. Use of either trademark requires the permission of International Bible Society.

All rights reserved. No part of this publication may be reproduced, stored in a retrieval system, or transmitted in any form or by any means—electronic, mechanical, photocopy, recording, or any other—except for brief quotations in printed reviews, without the prior permission of the author.

Published in the United States of America
by Obadiah Press

Dedication

Thank you, God, for giving me the courage to write this book; for giving me the words to write it and the resources to get it out into the world; and for your daily guidance and support in my life. I pray that *When A Woman Prays* will be the instrument you use to bring other women into your kingdom and into a closer, more personal relationship with you.

Table of Contents:

Foreword		13
Introduction		15
Chapter 1.	The Search	19
Chapter 2.	Getting to Know God	29
Chapter 3.	Teach Me to Pray	34
Chapter 4.	The Power of Prayer	58
Chapter 5.	Formal Prayer	72
Chapter 6.	Not So Formal Prayer	81
Chapter 7.	Praying for Others	87
Chapter 8.	Finding Forgiveness	98
Chapter 9.	God Answers Every Prayer	104
Chapter 10.	Listening For His Voice	115
Chapter 11.	Walking by Faith	120
Chapter 12.	Do Not Worry	130
Chapter 13.	Praying For Purpose	136
Chapter 14.	Abide in Me	145
Chapter 15.	The Miracles	151
Chapter 16.	The Journey	156
Resources:	Prayers	161
	People Who Want to Pray With You	166
	More Books on Prayer	168

Acknowledgments

There are many people who directly or indirectly helped make it possible for this book to be written. I am sure I will not be able to list them all, but I do want to acknowledge some of them here, because their support and contributions mean more than words can say—and I want to thank them for the way they have touched my life.

My parents, Delmer and Charlotte Schug, had me baptized as a baby, took me to church, taught me to pray, raised me to know and love God, and loved me as much as any two people can love a child—and they still do! I love you both!

My teachers, especially those at Maple Grove School—Lorraine Fehr, Ruth Boettcher, Bonnie Christianson (formerly Hinterleitner), and the late Doris Haas—taught me to read, write, and to have confidence in myself. Teachers, like parents, are some of the people we often take for granted, but each of you had a tremendous influence on my life.

My husband, John, and my children, David and Katarina, put up with the side effects of my writing—like my disappearing into my office for many long hours to write, paperwork spread all over the house, and eating whatever was fast and easy for supper! The three of you have also been my greatest fans. I love you all! I couldn't have done this without your support.

The Momwriters group provided support and

encouragement for my writing and cheered me on when I needed a lift. I've never known a stronger, more supportive group of women. You are all great!

My friend, LaDonna Meredith, had the dream of Obadiah Press and *Obadiah Magazine* and asked me to share it with her. God blessed me when He brought us together in faith to serve Him.

Many other important women in my life—friends and family—Ginger, Heather, Jackie, Sheila, Jolene, Linda, Tanya, Denise, Carolyn, Connie, Alyice, Koni, and others—have all been a support and an inspiration to me and frequently got neglected while I was busy writing. Even if I didn't have time to call as often as I would have liked because I lost track of time (yes, Ginger, that is for you, Baby Sis!), I appreciate all of your love and encouragement.

Blank page

My Prayer for You

Dear Heavenly Father,
Wrap your loving arms around this woman now before you. She holds this book in her hands because she is searching, Lord. Something is missing in her life. She is hurting, and she needs the peace and love that only you can give.

Your spirit brought her to this place and this moment—even prompted her to reach out and select this book to hold in her hands—or somehow brought this book to be given to her. There are no coincidences—only your divine guidance in keeping with your perfect—though often difficult for us as human beings to understand—plan.

Speak to her, dear God, with your words—your message—through this book. Whisper softly to her heart and soul, and stir her faith in you. Renew her hope, and share your joy with her.

This I ask in Jesus' name,
Amen

Foreword

Miracles can happen when a woman prays...miracles in the lives of the people she prays for, miracles in the lives of the people she loves, and miracles in her own life. Your miracle begins with you—and your relationship with God.

There is an incredible power inherent in prayer, and that power is available to all who will seek it in sincerity and faith. It is the awesome power of our loving and Almighty Father in heaven. It is the power of God.

My purpose in writing this book is to help you fill the emptiness in your life...in your soul. It is to help you develop and enjoy the most intimate and fulfilling relationship you will ever have—a relationship with God. It is simple and life changing. And it all begins with prayer.

This story is about a personal journey from childlike faith to doubt. About the struggle to fill the emptiness within. About realizing that only through God can we ever truly find fulfillment. About making a choice—through our own free will—to know and love Him. About finding the one—*The One*—who can fill the emptiness and love us unconditionally. And it is about developing a special, intimate, joyous relationship with God. Through prayer. It is my personal journey. And it is yours.

n recent years, I have felt a particular calling to motivate and inspire others through my writing and speaking. I believe this is a gift from God, and I have chosen to use this gift to share His love with others.

Particularly, I feel called to help other women come closer to God and discover His touch in their lives—to help them find the joy and happiness, peace and fulfillment that only He can bring them. I know what it is to be a woman—the longings, the struggles, and the feelings. I can relate to much of what you're going through, because I've been there. I'm still there. Life is a journey, not a destination. I will continue to learn as I fulfill my purpose in this life, but even though I don't yet have all the answers and probably never will, God is calling me to write this book right now. Prepared or not prepared, I must heed His call and His timing.

The idea for this book has been rolling around in my head and struggling to come out on paper for more than two years. I still don't feel qualified to write it. I can only hope and pray and trust in God that if I place this into His hands, He will help me to put the right words on the page and touch someone's soul, as He sees fit.

And so it is that I place this book into His hands and dedicate it to Him and the women whose lives He will touch with the words He helps me put on its pages.

Introduction

If you have never prayed before, the idea of praying may seem strange to you. You may wonder about people who pray, how they do it, what they say, and what they mean when they say their prayers are answered—particularly if bad things still seem to happen to them even after they have prayed.

You may not know how to pray. The idea may seem foreign, unusual, or uncomfortable—even kind of weird. Maybe it even scares you a bit. If you were to begin to pray, what would you say and how would you say it? You may have questions: Do I have to pray out loud? Do I have to memorize something? What if someone else is listening? What if I screw up? How do I know if my prayers are answered? How do I know anyone hears my prayers?

For those of you who have never prayed before, this book will help you with these questions and concerns.

***

Some of you have been praying your whole lives. But you wonder if you are praying the "right" way, if your prayers have been heard, or if your efforts are in vain. You want to grow in your spiritual life and become more confident in your faith. Perhaps you feel you have reached an impasse or feel rather desperate about a particular situation in your life. You want to be able to know, trust, and believe that your prayers are being heard and know they will be answered.

***

Maybe it just feels like something is missing when you pray or your heart is just not in it.

***

Let me begin by assuring you that there is no single right way to pray. Prayer is an individual thing. People in many different religions and denominations pray. Muslims pray to Allah, Buddhists pray to Buddha, Jews pray to God, and Christians pray to a triune God—often described as three parts, but one God—Father, Son, and Holy Spirit. Some Christians of particular denominations also say prayers to the Blessed Virgin Mary, who is the mother of Jesus, and to particular saints, asking them to intercede on their behalf and take their petitions to God.

I can only write from my experience and my beliefs. Just as prayer is a very personal thing for each individual, this story will be my personal story. It is my personal perspective on praying and prayer and the story of my journey in faith.

I believe in one God, who is three parts—Father, Son, and Holy Spirit. (For those of you who have difficulty with this concept, I once heard a wonderful analogy that helped it all make sense for me. Compare God with an egg. God has three parts—Father, Son, and Holy Spirit, but He is still only one God. An egg has three parts—white, yolk, and shell, but it is still only one egg.)

I believe the Lord Jesus Christ was born to a virgin, became man, suffered, was crucified, and died for my sins and the sins of all mankind, and was buried in a tomb. And I believe that on the third day after His crucifixion, He rose from the dead and ascended into heaven where today He sits at the right hand of God the Father. And because He died for me and my sins, and because I believe this, I will spend everlasting life in heaven with Him after I die.

I think it is important and relevant that you understand my views and my beliefs. Certainly, they will influence how I look at the concept of prayer. You should know this at the onset.

I will tell you up front that I do not have all the answers. Like many of you, I have made many mistakes in my lifetime and done many things I'm not very proud of.

I am not a Christian scholar or ordained minister. I know what I know from my own experiences and the lessons I learned along the way and from God's many blessings in my life. Many of the lessons I learned did not come easily. I often cried out to God, *"Why me, Lord? Why is this happening to me?"* Sometimes the answers were slow in coming because I did not understand God's plan for my life.

But I believe that in sharing my experience, I may be able to help someone else develop a closer, more personal relationship with God. I can't think of anything more wonderful than that.

If you do not share my beliefs, I invite you to read on with an open heart and an open mind. Something I say may strike a chord in you, ring true, or otherwise touch your soul. I pray that it will move you in some way.

If you are a Christian who believes as I do, I hope this book will enrich your prayer life and help you continue a little further along your own personal journey of faith. Perhaps something you read will inspire you and bring you just a little bit closer to God. If even one of you reads this and is touched in this way, then this book will have served its purpose.

Chapter 1: The Search

Growing Up With God

I was baptized as a baby and raised a Christian. As a child, I learned to love Jesus with all my heart and soul. It was pure and natural. I loved Him and believed in Him without question. My prayers were simple—words I had been taught to recite like the pure and simple words of the Lord's Prayer or the prayers I said before I went to sleep each night. Most of these prayers were simple requests to bless me and my family and to have His angels watch over us and guide our way.

The Seeds of Doubt

But as I began to grow and develop—sometime in my early teen years—my faith began to weaken. I didn't even know it at the time. But the ways of the outside world crept into my safe and secure little world. I heard about bad things that happened around the globe, and I couldn't understand why God allowed them to occur.

I began to question and doubt and to struggle with my beliefs. I looked at the outside world—in some ways so callous and cold—and I couldn't process it all. I didn't understand how God could allow the pain, the suffering, and the hatred. Murders and abductions, wars, and cruelty I could never have imagined were going on all over the earth. Why didn't He stop it? How could this be happening? My simple faith could not comprehend it.

Then some of these tragedies and horrible crimes hit our rural community and impacted my young life directly, and I *really* couldn't understand how God could let these things happen.

The seeds of doubt had been planted. The veil of innocence was lifted, and I found myself in the "real world."

While the ways of this world were not perfect, along with all the negative, scary, and unimaginable things, they held promises of beauty, happiness, love, contentment, satisfaction, wealth, and excitement. Everywhere I looked, I saw the promises—in books and magazines, on television and on billboards, in the songs I heard on the radio and the movies I went to see. There was a good world out there, too—a world where people were happy and content.

Something is Missing

Though I didn't abandon God entirely, a struggle had started inside me. I started looking for love and happiness in all the wrong places. It would take me many, many years to realize that what I was looking for couldn't be found in the outside world.

It's difficult to understand what I felt during those years—and sometimes I still feel a twinge of it—but I'm willing to bet you can understand it, because I'll bet you've felt it, too. It's kind of like an emptiness inside—a space that longs to be filled. It's a longing for someone who has the answers; someone who will know and love us; someone who thinks we are wonderful and needs us; someone who makes us feel good about ourselves;

someone who brings us joy and happiness, peace and contentment, a feeling of purpose and fulfillment; someone who will make our life complete.

We've spent our whole lives searching for that special someone to fill that emptiness. But we look and look in vain.

Our relationships are not all that we want them to be. They may begin in a whirlwind of romance and infatuation that makes us feel that we're on the right track, but sooner or later—and usually sooner—they fall apart. Our prince charming isn't really so charming after all. He lets us down or disappoints us. Or he decides we're not what he wanted and dumps us. Now we feel even more empty and wounded than we felt before.

Some of us become desperate. If we cannot fill that space with some*one*, we think that maybe we can fill it with some*thing*. And we try. Many of us in different ways, but so much the same. We're all trying to fill the same hole.

Searching for "Something"

We cannot find the love and fulfillment we're looking for. So we feel bad about ourselves. We feel let down. And in an effort to feel better or bring ourselves "up," we look outward. In a thousand different ways, we try to fill that emptiness.

For some it is shopping. A new dress or a pretty picture for our bedroom wall. A new living room set or just a little locket. Big or small, expensive or not, it will give us a nice lift, right? By purchasing this thing for ourselves, it will validate our self worth—or so we convince ourselves.

Maybe we get a makeover or a new hairstyle. We start exercising and lose 10 pounds—change our appearance in some way. If we look better, we will feel better about ourselves, and if we look and feel better, we will attract that certain, special someone who will fill that emptiness, right? Because it must be us. Something must certainly be wrong with us that we have not been able to attract that certain someone who will take all our worries away, make all our dreams come true, and give us that perfect feeling of fulfillment.

But it doesn't seem to work. So some of us give up on that approach and try another—perhaps we begin eating to escape. Because the food tastes good for a moment and it doesn't judge us or condemn us. It's always there when we want it, and it seems to soothe us, at least for a while. And in time, it insulates us and protects us from the outside world—a layer of fat between our inner emptiness and the outside world that will not give us the love and acceptance we want. Now no one can get in and hurt us.

Some turn to alcohol or drugs. The high may not last, but for the time that it does, it makes us feel good—or so we convince ourselves—and it numbs us to the pain we really feel—that awful sense that somehow we are not good enough or worthy enough of being loved. It is an escape from dealing with the emptiness.

Others of us think we're stronger than all that. We are in control of our own lives, and we can turn it around. We will simply make the life we want. We'll create it. We're smart and capable women. Who says we need a man? We can build a life and a lifestyle that is personally satisfying and fulfilling. So we get a good education, work hard, climb the ladder of success, and arrive: Where? All those years of goal setting, sacrifice, hard work, and perseverance, and we find that even after we have achieved all of this, it does not fill the emptiness inside.

Some women fell in love—convinced we had found the person who would make us feel completely happy, worthy, and fulfilled—married and had a family, settled down and turned a house or apartment into a home, and—for better or worse—tried to live a good life. Yet still, even though we have everything we said we ever wanted, our life is not complete. Something is missing.

Some of us spend our whole lives searching. Searching for that elusive "something" that will make us feel complete. We look for the perfect man to make us feel loved, the ideal career to make us feel fulfilled, children and a family to make us feel complete, hobbies and pursuits to make us feel content, a place to call home.

Yet even women who attain all of these things that are symbolic of a meaningful, happy life find they are still missing "something."

That elusive "something." Money can't buy it. Fame and fortune can't find it. The most creative women can't design it. And no other human being can give it to us.

Discontentment

One day you wake up and ask yourself: "Is this all that there is?" You've been living your life day by day, making the best decisions you can under the circumstances you're given and trying to be a good person. Sure, you've made mistakes along the way, but who hasn't? Still, you expected your life to be different somehow...

Despite the fact that your days are packed full of activities from dawn til dark and then some, you can't seem to find that sense of real fulfillment. You have a good life, and you really shouldn't complain, right? After all, there are lots of other women out there who would give their right arm for the life you have.

And while you have your troubles—who doesn't—if you had to exchange problems with anyone else, you know you'd be satisfied to just deal with your own.

It gnaws at you sometimes—that sense of discontent. You wonder if a change in career or lifestyle would make a difference. You gaze at the grass on the other side of the fence and envy the lives of women who look like they have it so much better than you.

If you are a stay-at-home mom with small children, you stare with envy at the women who get dressed up each day to go to work in a fancy office.

If you work outside the home to help support your family, you struggle to balance your job, family, and personal life and are convinced that your life would be so much easier and better if only you didn't have to work.

Married women listen to the stories of dating and romance their single friends tell and wonder what ever happened to the romance in their lives. *Oh, to be single again*, they think.

While meanwhile the single women ache with loneliness for that special someone who will love them enough to marry them.

It doesn't matter where you live or what you do, whether you are a single woman or married, divorced or widowed, childless or a mother…sooner or later we all ask ourselves, "Is this all there is?"

We can clearly see the ways our lives may be better than those of thousands of other women in the world today. Chances are we are not starving or without clothing or shelter, and while we may have bad days and irritating bosses, neighbors, or husbands, most of us are not being persecuted. We start to feel kind of selfish for wanting more and we try to stuff those feelings down inside.

Yet still we feel the ache of emptiness within.

We Want it All

How much more do we want? Society tells us we can "have it all." Magazines tout images of beautiful models with seemingly perfect bodies, gorgeous hair, and an almost magnetic attraction that draws men to them like bees to honey and makes all of us insanely jealous of the women in the photos.

We grew up on fairy tales and romantic movies and expected our adult lives to be like that, and when we finally realized that "happily ever after" is a myth, the depression and discouragement set in. Some of us may have even learned the hard way—thinking the husband or boyfriend we had was the problem and trading him in on a new model—only to find out that it's not the man, but the mindset that is the problem. We are expecting to live a fantasy, and fantasies just don't exist.

We get discouraged and frustrated when we find out there is no such thing as the perfect relationship, perfect family, perfect career, perfect us.

Even surrounded by people, we feel isolated and alone. Something is most definitely missing, and we don't know what it is.

Have you ever heard the phrase "looking for love in all the wrong places?" Well, if one could sum up the total of what is wrong in our lives, that would probably describe the problem to a "T".

As women, we bought into the hype—women's lib, equal rights, and/or the "you can have it all" mentality. "I am woman, hear me roar!" Remember?

Making Choices

The plain and simple fact is, it's not possible to have it all, and anyone who tells you that you can is full of beans. Life is about choices. You cannot have your cake and eat it, too. You must make decisions.

Throughout our lives, in our search for happiness and joy, we've made our choices—some for better and some for worse. We've made poor choices and hopefully learned from our mistakes. We've made some good choices and enjoyed the rewards, too.

But when we get to this point in our lives, we begin to question *all* the choices we made along the way. We become convinced that "if only" we had made different choices, our lives would be better, more meaningful, happier. "If only, if only."

But it's not necessarily the choices we made that got us into the rut we're in today—at least not in the sense that you're thinking. The truth is, whether we chose to marry or stay single, have children or pursue a career, go to college or get a job, it doesn't really matter. Eventually we would all get to this point—discontented and looking for that elusive something that is missing.

There are a million different variations possible, and one of them is you. Whether you consider yourself successful or a failure, basically happy or desperately miserable, healthy or sick, rich or poor, worthy or unworthy, you still feel an emptiness inside that you have been unable to fill. Until now.

Filling Your Emptiness

Today you will begin to fill the emptiness inside and to achieve all that you truly need. But it will not be with worldly promises...or magic...or a special diet...or a new car...or a high-limit credit card...or a pill...or any of a thousand other things the world has to offer.

It will not cost you a cent. It is not a secret.

You can begin now to find the peace, love, and acceptance you've been longing for.

It is simple and freely available to all who want it. You can begin to have it right now, this very moment. You do not need to dress for the occasion or wait for the right moment or go to a particular place. You don't have to lose 10 pounds first, and you won't need an appointment.

Your fulfillment begins now—at the very moment you decide to begin a deep and meaningful relationship with God.

You see, that elusive something you've been searching for all this time is *unconditional love* and there is only one place you can get it: *God*. God is and has always been the only being capable of loving us unconditionally and without question despite our sinful nature, our mistakes, and our faults. No one else ever could or ever will compare. Our husbands, our children, our friends, and our jobs can all fill a *part* of our lives, but they can never fill it completely. Even stacked on top of one another, all of them together cannot make us feel whole.

Only God can.

We have been looking for love in all the wrong places—in people and places who cannot give us the unconditional love we so need and desire.

We need to turn to God.

☦ Do you feel something missing from your life?
☦ Do you feel confused and alone?
☦ Does the idea of being alone scare you?
☦ Have you tried to fill feelings of loneliness or emptiness with worldly things that just don't fulfill you?
☦ Are you busier than you've ever been but still feel like your life lacks something?
☦ Are you scared that you may never find true happiness?

Pray With Me...

Dear Lord,
I often feel lonely and confused. Something is missing in my life, and I've tried so many ways to find it.

Sometimes I thought I'd found happiness, but it never seemed to last. I know now that I've been searching in all the wrong places and what I really need is you.

I want to feel your peace in my heart. Help me turn to you, and fill my emptiness with your love.

Amen

Chapter 2:
Getting to Know God

Do You Know Him?

Perhaps you don't really know God. Maybe He has never been a real and living part of your daily life. What if He seems distant to you?

You know, many people have vague or erroneous perceptions of God. Perhaps their impressions were formed in childhood or influenced by other events in their life. But however those impressions developed, they may think God is a distant being, harsh and judging, too busy to be bothered with our petty concerns, or that because we have not lived perfect lives, He will not want anything to do with us.

We need to cast some of those misconceptions or prejudices aside and get to know God ourselves—on an intimate, deeply personal level.

Spending Time with Him

When a woman falls in love with a man, she typically goes out of her way to find out as much as she can about him. She will follow him around and listen to him as he talks to his friends, discover his interests, find out what his favorite foods are and try to impress him by cooking them for him, and in other ways focus herself almost exclusively on him. Essentially, what it all comes down to is that we spend time with the people we love and we talk with them and get to know them. Time flies by and minutes turn into hours in their presence.

So it is when you develop a personal relationship with God. You must spend time with Him, talk with Him, listen for His answers and guidance, read about Him, talk about Him, and share yourself with Him. In turn, He will share Himself with you and a close, personal, loving relationship is born.

How do you begin that kind of a relationship with God if you have never had it before? Where do you start? How do you get to know Him?

I'd like to suggest that there are three important ways you can get to know God. All of them involve spending time with Him and in His presence.

1. Read His Word

You can read about God and follow His word in the Bible. The Bible is sometimes hard to understand, even for Biblical scholars, but it is also an endless source of wisdom and inspiration! The answers to all of life's questions are right there in that one book. It is truly amazing. If you are new to the Bible, start with the Good News messages that contain hope for your life today and direction and guidance on how to live your life effectively. Read the Gospel messages in the books of Matthew, Mark, Luke, and John.

The Good News messages of salvation in the New Testament tell us the complete story of God's incredible love and forgiveness and replace "the law" of the Old Testament.

Within this book, we will reflect on some quotations from Scripture that are particularly relevant, as well. Perhaps they will help you begin to appreciate and understand the wonderful insights the Bible reveals.

2. Join A Community of Believers

I encourage you to also attend worship services at a church in your area to learn more about God the Father; His Son, Jesus; and the Holy Spirit. Here you can learn from ministers and others who have spent years studying God's word, and you can hear the Good News proclaimed.

You will enjoy the support and fellowship of other Christians who can help you on your journey. Try several different Christian churches, if necessary, until you find one that feels like "home," and then join the church and become an active part of a community of believers. Your Christian friends can become a loving part of your extended family.

While there are some Christian believers who do not regularly attend church services, just as there are people who attend church services who really don't seem to be getting a whole lot out of the experience, I think you will find belonging to a Christian community an important part of your spiritual growth.

Regular worship and quiet time in a chapel or church helps nourish your spirit and provides the strength you need to face the challenges you face each day. Fellowship with other Christians renews your commitment and encourages you to be the best person you can be. Don't overlook church attendance and involvement as an opportunity for you to grow in your faith and make some good Christian friends in the process.

3. Pray

Last, but certainly not least and perhaps even first, you can pray. Pray to God, get to know Him, share yourself with Him, and develop a close, personal relationship with your Creator.

That is what this book is all about—learning how to pray, discovering why prayer is so important in your life, and helping you tune in to the miracles prayer will reveal to you.

You will find your life most deeply touched and affected when you do all three: read God's word in the Bible, join a church community of believers, *and* pray to God from your heart. You will also come to know and understand God much better when you seek Him in all three ways.

- ✟ Did you grow up with God in your life?
- ✟ If not, what do you imagine God is like?
- ✟ If so, what did you think God was like as a child? What do you think God is like now that you are older?
- ✟ Do you know God as well as you'd like?
- ✟ Do you spend time with Him on a daily basis like you do with your other loved ones?
- ✟ Do you want to spend more time with Him?
- ✟ Do you read God's word to learn more about Him?
- ✟ Do you spend time with other believers?
- ✟ Are you anxious to develop a more personal, intimate relationship with God?

Pray With Me...

Dear Lord,
I want to get to know you and to have a special, personal relationship with you. I want you to be a part of my life every day, in every way.

Please guide me to spend time with you every day, to read and understand your word, and to spend time with other Christians who will help me learn even more about you and grow in my faith.

Help me learn to pray to you from my heart.
Amen

Chapter 3:
Teach me to Pray

How Do I Pray?

How do I pray? I can hear some of you saying. *What is the "right" way to pray? You ask. I've been praying, but God never seems to answer my prayers,* a few of you despair ou despair.

Some people seem to think you need some special skill or talent to pray well. But that simply isn't true. You don't need a degree from a seminary or any fancy written words to pray. In fact, it's just the opposite. Jesus tells us to become like little children.

And he said, "I tell you the truth, unless you change and become like little children, you will never enter the kingdom of heaven. Therefore, whoever humbles himself like this child is the greatest in the kingdom of heaven." Matthew 18:3-4

In other words, take away all the fancy stuff and the "image," all the airs we put on for other people, the act we perform every day, and the face we show the world. Humble yourself and speak from your heart and soul. Say what is on your mind. Tell Him what you're thinking.

Are you scared? Sad? Anxious or worried? Take it to the Lord in prayer! Do you feel happy and joyful? Has something wonderful happened? Share it with the Lord! Thank Him for blessing you and your life. Do you need help, guidance, or direction? Are you unsure of yourself? Who better to direct your steps than the Creator of all things? The one and only being with a master plan? The God of all? Go to Him and ask Him to help you do His will.

Are you fearful—of someone, something, or perhaps the unknown? Be not afraid, God tells us.

...If God is for us, who can be against us? Romans 8:31

With God on our side, what more could we ask for? We know that come what may, everything will be all right.

Begin Where You Are

How then do you begin to pray? Very simply, you just start. Find some time when you can be alone with God—away from the distractions of the world. Turn off the television and radio or other things that might distract you. Escape into a quiet room, a church, or a secluded spot outdoors. If you have small children, wait until the children are asleep and soak in a nice hot bathtub filled with bubbles.

"...when you pray, go into your room, close the door and pray to your Father, who is unseen." Matthew 6:6

Go into a quiet place and try to empty the thoughts from your mind as much as you can. If something is troubling you, this may be difficult to do. But tell yourself that you will think about it in a moment and try to set it aside briefly.

Close your eyes and breathe slowly. Relax and try to feel God's presence. You are with God and God is with you. God's presence feels like a gentle settling of your soul. It is a peaceful moment, a quiet stillness, and a feeling of well being. When you experience this, you are feeling God's presence.

If you cannot feel it, do not be alarmed. God is not absent from your life. He is right there with you, ever present and always. But you may not be used to speaking with God. Though He knows you intimately, you may not be familiar with Him.

Try to drain the tension from your mind and body and begin. Talk to God in your mind—or even out loud if that is comfortable for you. Speak to Him in your own language, in your own way. Whatever way you are most comfortable communicating, God will get the message.

Talk to Him

Just start talking to Him. It may feel funny at first—you may find yourself soaking in a bathtub full of bubbles thinking, *OK, God. Here I am. I have no clue what I should say to you or why I am doing this, but I just know that there is something missing in my life right now and I have come to the conclusion that those feelings of emptiness probably have a lot to do with you. I've never prayed before (or I haven't prayed to you in a long time), but I want to have a close, personal relationship with you in my life. I am ready for a change and I'm going to need your help.*

My prayers are very simply one-on-one conversations with God. I talk with Him about everything—sometimes I just tell Him about my day. I talk to Him the same way I would talk to a close friend. Often I share any concerns I might have, and sometimes I just pour my heart out to Him.

At some point during these conversations with Him, I try to focus on all the blessings I've been given and thank Him for all the wonderful things He has done in my life. I reflect on the ways I may have pleased Him or let Him down since I spoke with Him last and ask Him to help me to do better in the future.

When I am pondering a decision, I can turn to Him for guidance and direction and listen quietly for His wisdom to come to me. Sometimes I also read the Bible to try to discern His will and find my way.

While I firmly believe a person can truly pray anywhere—and I do pray in some very strange as well as very traditional locations—it may be the easiest for women who are first beginning to pray and seeking to develop a more intimate, personal prayer life to find a secluded spot of their own—even if it is in a tub full of bubbles—to be alone with God (hopefully) uninterrupted. It's easier to focus.

Starting to Pray

At first you may feel like you are talking to the wall, but be assured, you are not. Whether talking to God in your mind and heart or praying out loud, God hears you and He will answer!

It may be hard for you at first to imagine that God is up there listening to you right now and that with all of the millions of creatures on this planet, He can give you His undivided attention. Your faith may be weak at first and you may have a hard time with this concept. It can be difficult to understand something you cannot see or touch.

Did you know that it is OK to ask God to strengthen your faith? Did you know that He will welcome your communication with Him even if you are still struggling?

Your first prayer to God may well be a prayer to help you pray! And despite your initial reservations or doubts, God *will* help increase your faith and give you the knowledge you need to pray. Just try it and see. God is only too happy to help you.

God is just so overjoyed that you are talking to Him! My goodness, do you know how long He's been waiting for you?

Don't Wait! Pray Today

Some women think it is "too late" for them to develop a relationship with God. They may not feel worthy of God's love. Perhaps they are ashamed of something they did or thought—or something they didn't do.

***

Some women don't come to God in prayer because they think they can do it all themselves. They are independent, self-sufficient, and they don't need anyone—even God. Maybe especially God—until their world comes crashing down around them. Perhaps they lose a loved one due to death or divorce. Or they are diagnosed with a serious illness. They lose their job or their home or they are physically attacked. Or they become addicted to pills or alcohol or develop an eating disorder in their quest for perfection. Whatever the case, these women have to reach rock bottom before they finally realize there is nowhere else to go but to God.

***

In all these circumstances, too, God is simply overjoyed that you finally turned to Him. The past doesn't matter anymore.

Imagine Him up there, this loving, tender Father of Mercy looking down upon you with tears in His eyes and arms outstretched to pick you up and hold you close to Him. "At last," He murmurs gently, wiping away your tears. "At last you came to me."

"I have been waiting for you for so long…"

***

God will wait, you know. He will not force Himself into our lives.

The Gift of Free Will

From the very beginning when God first made Adam and Eve, He gave people their own free will—choices. He wanted us to love and honor Him and to invite Him into our hearts and our lives. But He always made it our choice, our decision.

Perhaps some of the things that happen in our lives are orchestrated by God to test us or "break us"—to enable us to get to the point where we must face the fact that we can't do it alone, on our own—to make us realize we *need* God in our lives. That is not for me to say although the thought crosses my mind sometimes.

Perhaps the suffering we endure is simply a natural and logical consequence of the choices we make in this life and the mistakes we inevitably make along the way because we are only human. And because all too often we *don't* call on God to help us make our daily choices and decisions.

The point is, all of God's kingdom is made up of sinners. None of us—despite any outward appearances to the contrary—are without sin. It should never be a matter of not praying—not starting to pray—because we don't feel "good enough" to come to Him. *None* of us are deserving of His love and forgiveness. None of us are "good enough" to have a special, personal relationship with God. All of us have fallen short in our lives. And He doesn't care. He *wants* us to come to Him anyway—flaws and all. There is nothing God would like better than if every one of us came to Him.

Ask For Forgiveness

Despite your failures and sins, go to God in prayer. Tell Him about the things you regret, the poor choices or decisions you've made, and how badly you feel about your sinfulness. Humble yourself before him and simply ask Him to forgive you for your faults and failings. If you are sincere, this is one of the best ways to start a prayer to God. Admit that you are not worthy of His goodness and grace and then thank Him that He gives it to you in spite of it.

Thank Him for Jesus' suffering on our behalf and His incredible gift of grace, mercy, and forgiveness freely given to each of us. Make a commitment to move forward in sincere repentance and to try to live a better life. Ask Him to bless you and help you live a life that will be pleasing to Him.

Commit to making a fresh, clean start and to creating a life that will glorify and honor Him.

He Waits For You

Regardless of the circumstances that kept us away from God or led us to distance ourselves from Him and regardless of the circumstances that lead us back in His direction, it is still up to us to invite Him into our lives.

God places His Holy Spirit in our hearts to prompt us to welcome Him—to prepare our hearts for Him. But we must ask Him in.

"Here I am! I stand at the door and knock. If anyone hears my voice and opens the door, I will come in and eat with him, and he with me." Revelations 3:20

God loves us and wants to spend time with us. He wants us to spend time with Him. But He will not force Himself on us. We must come to Him, willingly and openly, and ask to receive Him in our lives. That's what the gift of choice is all about.

And when we do come to Him and invite Him into our hearts, He will be there for us always.

"Ask and it will be given to you; seek and you will find; knock and the door will be opened to you. For everyone who asks receives; he who seeks finds; and to him who knocks, the door will be opened." Matthew 7:7-8

Whatever gets us to this point hardly matters anymore. The important thing is, we're here. We realize we need God and want Him to be a part of our lives.

And He is overjoyed.

Speechless in His Presence

There really are no "right" words to use when you pray. Simply speak to God from your heart. Talk to Him, communicate with Him, and share your thoughts and your life with Him. He wants you to tell him what is on your mind, how you feel, your fears and uncertainties. He is there for you when you are scared and unsure to comfort you and help reassure you. No matter what it is, He wants you to come to Him—He wants to be your lifeline. He wants to know that you need Him and love Him and trust Him to help you.

When words fail us, God provides.

...the Spirit helps us in our weakness. We do not know what we ought to pray for, but the Spirit himself intercedes for us with groans that words cannot express. And he who searches our hearts knows the mind of the Spirit, because the Spirit intercedes for the saints in accordance with God's will. Romans 8:26-27

A Perfect God for Imperfect People

When you pray, talk to God as if you were talking to a good friend. God is really and truly your very best friend. He loves you like no one else ever has, ever will, or even can. He loves you unconditionally, knowing all of your faults and flaws in intimate detail, and yet loving you anyway.

God knows you better than anyone. He knows your thoughts, your dreams, your fears. He has known you intimately since the beginning of time.

"Before I formed you in the womb I knew you..." Jeremiah 1:5

God loves you just the way you are—sins and all. But He loves you too much to leave you that way.

He loves you so much that He sacrificed His one and only Son to a painful, humiliating death on the cross just so that you might live eternally with Him in heaven.

You don't have to be perfect to come before God. And He knows you cannot become perfect because you are only human. Starting to pray will not make you perfect either. And *not* being perfect should not deter you from praying and seeking Him.

God knows we are not perfect. That is why He sent His one and only Son to die for us, to save us from our sins. He knows we could not save ourselves. We were born as sinful beings.

We will stumble and fall along our path to Him. We will take wrong turns in the road. But if we ask Him, He will also be there to help guide our steps and direct us in His way. When we confess our sinfulness and repent of our mistakes, He will forgive us, wipe away our sins, and actually forget about them! Though human beings may remember, God will not.

"...Though your sins are like scarlet, they shall be as white as snow..." Isaiah 1:18

Once our sins are forgiven, they are forgiven and they are washed away. Incredible!

True prayer comes from the heart and the soul, not a textbook or pre-written script. We are not actors in our lives. Saying the "right" words isn't important; talking with Him is.

Miracles Await You

Miracles happen when a woman prays—miracles in the people and the world around her and miracles in the woman herself. Prayer puts you in touch with God's grace, His wisdom, and His understanding.

Real Communication

Prayer is, very simply, communication with God. It is the act of communicating your thoughts, feelings, questions, and concerns *to* God and the act of listening for His response.

Does this mean that God will speak to you in a voice of thunder or audibly pronounce His reply in a voice the whole world can hear? No.

Sometimes we almost wish He would. I've often joked that if He could send me a burning bush or some other visible *sign* like in old Biblical times that it would make discerning His will much easier. But that's not the way He does it these days.

Nonetheless, if you listen closely, He will speak to you. He will speak to your soul. He will touch your life in a thousand miraculous little ways each and every day.

Prayer can be during a quiet moment or in the midst of the rush of the day. It does not matter where you are or what you are doing. It does not matter who you are or who you are with. It does not matter your language or your creed. God hears all prayers. And God answers all prayers. God loves each of us individually and specially. We are His children and He wants to have a loving, mutually responsive relationship with each and every one of us. He has called out to us a million times in a million little ways. Have you heard Him?

Will you answer?

Prayer does not require much from you, but that special

relationship you will form with God offers so much in return. Prayer requires only honesty, sincerity, faith, hope, and love.

Honesty

Some of us spend our whole lives lying to ourselves. Perhaps we pretend that we are 10 pounds thinner than we really are. Or "forget" to change the number on our driver's license when we renew it even though we know its been years since we weighed 110 pounds. We put on our best faces for our friends and the people we meet. We want to leave a good impression.

But deep down inside we know that we are really sinful. We know the awful things we have done or said or thought, the countless ways we have hurt others or failed to help them, the selfish or hateful feelings we've had, and all of our flaws can seem overwhelming. Sometimes we turn that pain—the pain of knowing ourselves truly and honestly with all our faults—into a kind of self-loathing. We "punish" ourselves in a thousand different ways—by putting ourselves down or telling ourselves that we are not worthy of God's love.

We hold ourselves to worldly illusions of perfection and success—seeking to achieve the perfect figure, hairstyle, clothes, and makeup. We set ourselves up for failure as we attempt to be someone we're not. We think that if we can somehow achieve this thing we call "perfection," we can be worthy of or find this unconditional love we so crave.

Like Adam and Eve in the garden, we try to hide. We hide our sins from the rest of the world. We hide our sins from ourselves, burying them deep in our hearts where they fester and burn, and we try to hide them from God.

But the truth is, we cannot hide from God. We cannot tell God anything He does not already know. He knows everything. Our very deepest thoughts and desires. Our best self. Our most shameful self. The woman you are and the woman you want to be. He sees your flaws and He loves you anyway.

There is nothing you can tell God that He doesn't already know. Believe me, you cannot shock God. He's heard it all and He's seen it all.

God knows everything about us—even the number of hairs on our head. *"And even the very hairs on your head are all numbered..."* Matthew 10:30

He knows what is in our heart—the good and the bad. He knows all about our sins and our failings—and He loves us anyway!

***

God loves us just the way we are, but He loves us *too* much to leave us that way. He wants more for us—everlasting life, complete unconditional love, happiness, peace, and joy—even more than the blessings we want for our children. If you are a mother, think of how much you love your own children—how fiercely and intensely you want to love and protect them. Now multiply that a million times over and you will begin to feel something of what God wants for us, His children.

We can and must be open and honest with God—lay it all on the line—the sorrow, the pain, the frustration, the things we've done and failed to do, our thoughts and actions, the dark side of us, the things we're ashamed of—in honesty and humble attrition. Bring it all to Him and lay it at His feet. He knows it all anyway. We *can't shock Him*. But we must admit our sins to Him and to ourselves—so we can release them and accept His gift of forgiveness and begin anew, washed clean by His love and by the sacrifice of His son for us.

***

Sometimes I try to comprehend how much He loves us. I know how much I love my own children—fiercely, intensely, like no one else—God loves us that much and more. He also loved His son, Jesus, that much and more. And still He sacrificed His only son on the cross for us. Can you imagine watching your son suffer and die—and such a horrible death, deliberately inflicted by others, too? I can't. It hurts too much to even think of such a thing. And yet He did.

***

We don't ever have to pretend with God. He understands. And when we try to whitewash our lives for Him, justify our actions that we know were wrong, rationalize our feelings according to the ways of the world, etc., He can see right through us. To even try only puts up a barrier between us and God.

But if we come to Him honestly sorry for our actions, He will forgive us *anything* we have done. Incredible. Unimaginable. God's way.

And as if that gift of forgiveness is not enough, our awesome and incredible God takes it a step further. When we come to Him in total humble and contrite honesty to receive His blessing of acceptance, love and forgiveness, and a fresh, clean start, the Bible tells us He washes away our sins and even forgets all about them.

This perfect God who can do all things *chooses* to forget all about our transgressions when we are truly sorry for them and gives us the only truly brand new start there is. No one else could ever do that. People can forgive, but they seldom forget. God does—but not because of a memory lapse or some other imperfection, for He has none, but because He *chooses* to.

***

Despite all of our imperfections, we can go to God honestly and humbly just the way we are—with all our faults. His strength is made perfect in our weakness.

"...My grace is sufficient for you, for my power is made perfect in weakness." Therefore I will boast all the more gladly about my weaknesses, so that Christ's power may rest on me. 2 Corinthians 12:9

Where we lack, He supplies all our needs. When we are weak, we can draw from His strength. He holds us up with His everlasting arms.

"The eternal God is your refuge and underneath are the everlasting arms..." Deuteronomy 33:27

We can run and not grow weary.

But those who hope in the Lord will renew their strength. They will soar on wings like eagles. They will run and not grow weary. They will walk and not be faint. Isaiah 40:31

***

Ever hear that saying—God never gives us more than we can handle? Well, it's true—with a little caveat. He never gives us more than we can handle *with* Him—with His help and strength to carry us through. But we can't handle the troubles of this life on our own. We need Him.

***

How do people who don't have God to lean on get through the tough times, the difficult days, even the "normal" everyday days? I don't know. Maybe that's why so many of them don't. Some give up.

Some of us find God when we finally realize and are forced to admit we cannot do it alone. Difficulties or troubles are finally the catalyst that draws us to Him. We finally find our way there on our knees.

Maybe we get too self-assured, too cocky and confident, too independent out on our own when things seem to be going well, and we start to think we can do it alone. We start to take credit for our success when it is not our credit to take. It is His. He blesses us and sustains us in ways that *allow* us to succeed.

Sometimes we need to be reminded who should get the glory. When we pray, we are often reminded and must acknowledge that God is the divine force behind our blessings and success.

***

Prayer is most effective when you can totally and honestly communicate with God without pretense. It breaks down all the barriers. When we become like little children and humbly bring ourselves and all that we are before God, He welcomes us with open and loving arms, gathering us in an embrace like the loving Father He is. And He whispers in our soul the things that we need to know. All we have to do is come to Him in honesty and listen to His response in our lives.

Sincerity

We all want to be well liked. We want to be popular and attractive, known as a friendly person with a good heart. We spend our entire lives doing for others—sometimes with a pure heart and other times with an angry heart full of resentment—trying to get people's approval. We do things we do not want to do in the hope that it will someday bring us the desires of our hearts and the approval of other people.

Sometimes we even try to "earn" our way into heaven with our good deeds, reasoning that, though we are sinful, we can "make up" for our sins with our good works and good deeds.

But God does not require this kind of performance. God knows the real you and loves you anyway. You cannot win His love and affection with good deeds or by saying nice things—to Him or to anyone else. Any good that you do in this world should be out of sincere love and adoration for God and a desire to give something back in response to all the blessings He has already given you.

You could not earn your way into heaven no matter how long and hard you tried or what you did. It simply is not possible. We are human, and as humans, we are inherently sinful. But Jesus paid the price for us and for our sins when He died on the cross. His sacrifice is what assures us of eternal life with God.

"For it is by grace you have been saved, through faith—and this not from yourselves, it is the gift of God—not by works, so that no one can boast." Ephesians 2:8-9

Any good that we do in our lifetime should be done to honor and glorify God because we love Him and to bring praise to Him.

"In the same way, let your light shine before men, that they may see your good deeds and praise your Father in heaven." Matthew 5:16

He has called us to do His work according to His will— *For we are God's workmanship, created in Christ Jesus to do good works, which God prepared in advance for us to do.* Ephesians 2:10

Our good works should be done with praise and thanksgiving for the blessings we already receive and to set an example to others of how to lead a Godly life.

In everything set them an example by doing what is good... Titus 2:7

So when you pray, speak to God from the heart. Be sincere and earnest in your prayers. Don't put on airs with God. Tell Him what and how you really feel. Don't pretend to be something you're not. Heck, He already knows you're not perfect. There is no point is playing self-righteous with Him.

Do not pray the way you think you are "supposed to" using certain words and phrases. Do not imagine that you have to be eloquent or articulate. Don't worry at all about what you say. Just go to Him and bare your soul. Tell it like it is. Share your hurts and sorrows and the pain in your life. Ask Him to heal you. Thank Him for the blessings you've received. Talk to Him like a friend.

God is your friend, you know. He is your very best friend and no one can ever take His place in your life. All these things you have been searching for in the world can be found in Him.

***

You don't have to pretend to be anything at all when you pray to God. You are you. And that's all you need to be. He loves you because of all you are and in spite of what you do or do not do and there is nothing you will ever do that will change His love for you.

So be sincere. Be yourself. Out in the world, we all put on our little "acts." Sometimes we are proper and efficient, we try to be in control, and perhaps we put up a brave front trying to look tough. But with God, we can let all of our guards down and just be who we are.

Sometimes that may be a scared little girl who doesn't know what to do. That's OK. God understands. When you think no one else in the world does, He does and He always will.

You may be terrified about your own health, finances, something a family member or child is going through. Perhaps you are going through a divorce, bankruptcy, or grieving for a loved one. He is the source of all the love and comfort you need during any crisis in your life. Go to Him with your hurting heart.

Faith

"*Have faith in God,*" *Jesus answered. "I tell you the truth, if anyone says to this mountain, 'Go, throw yourself into the sea,' and does not doubt in his heart but believes what he says will happen, it will be done for him. Therefore I tell you, whatever you ask for in prayer, believe that you have received it, and it will be yours."* Mark 11:22-24

"*If you believe, you will receive whatever you ask for in prayer.*" Matthew 21:22

What wonderful passages from the Bible. What a blessed promise. There are times when we pray to God for something that seems nearly impossible. But as our faith is, so shall our prayers be answered.

"*...I tell you the truth, if you have faith as small as a mustard seed, you can say to this mountain, 'Move from here to there' and it will move. Nothing will be impossible for you.*" Matthew 17:20

Nothing is impossible with God. "*...with God all things are possible.*" Matthew 19:26

It's incredible and beyond our imagination. Who could make such a promise? That whatever we desire and ask Him for in prayer, that if we just believe He can and will provide it, that it will be? We shall have it. It is hard for us to even imagine that. But that is just exactly what God promises. Only He could make such a promise. Only God.

Only God could promise such a thing and be true to His word. And is. He has done wondrous and miraculous things time and time again.

Yet still we doubt. It is human, I suppose. But if we could just get past that doubting, all things would be given to us. Heartfelt prayer is boundless. It knows no limits. It abounds in miracles. The only thing that holds us back is our lack of faith. If you believe it, so it shall be.

So when you pray, do not burden God with your preconceived notions about what can and cannot be done. Do not limit Him with your conditions and guidelines. Do not impose human restrictions on the Great I Am. If your faith is weak, pray for more faith.

"So I say to you: Ask and it will be given to you; seek and you will find; knock and the door will be opened to you. For everyone who asks receives; he who seeks finds; and to him who knocks, the door will be opened." Luke 11:9

Believe that God will answer your prayers and He will. Pray in thanksgiving for answers to your needs in anticipation of those prayers being answered.

Let us then approach the throne of grace with confidence, so that we may receive mercy and find grace to help us in our time of need.
Hebrews 4:16

***

Faith is believing in something you cannot see. Though you cannot see the Living God and point to Him physically, yet you believe.

We live by faith, not by sight.
2 Corinthians 5:7

Hope

Like faith, hope must sustain us. God does answer all prayers. There has never been a prayer He has not heard. There has never been a prayer He has not answered. But He is God and we are human. God's ways are not our ways. We have all these expectations about *how* God should answer our prayers, how things should go, and how He will respond.

He will always answer our prayers, but not always in the way we expect Him to. Sometimes His answer is a blessed and immediate "yes." People often say their prayers have been answered when they receive an affirmative response from the Father.

But God is just as lovingly answering our prayers when he tells us "no" or "not yet, wait a while," too. Just because things do not go precisely the way *we* had planned does not mean that God is not working *His* plan in our lives—and a far better plan than any we could ever come up with.

It is sometimes hard to trust when we do not see an immediate, positive response to our prayer requests or the difficulties in our lives. It can be frustrating and scary. Therein lies hope.

We must have hope in all things and in all circumstances and in God. God's way will prevail. He is all powerful. He has a plan. And while we may not understand it every step of the way, and we may *never* understand it this side of heaven, He knows what He is doing.

And that should be enough.

Love

All real prayers must begin and end in love. Love is the only real way to pray.

...If I speak in the tongues of men and of angels, but have not love, I am only a resounding gong or a clanging cymbal. 1 Corinthians 13:1

...and if I have a faith that can move mountains, but have not love, I am nothing. 1 Corinthians 13:2

And now these three remain: faith, hope and love. But the greatest of these is love. 1 Corinthians 13:13

Your faith and hope may be weak. That's OK. We all go through ups and downs—times when our faith and hope are stronger than at other times. We can pray and ask God to strengthen our faith and give us hope. If real, pure love is in our heart and soul, we are connected to God. God is love. If we have love in us, we have God in us. It all starts right here.

Jesus replied, "Love the Lord your God with all your heart and with all your soul and with all your mind." This is the first and greatest commandment. And the second is like it: "Love your neighbor as yourself." Matthew 22:37-39

Our deep and abiding love for God must rule all our prayers. To "pray" with a false and insincere mindset is simply not possible. True prayer requires us to recognize and proclaim our dependence on the one God who created us out of His love. We were created in God's image. God is love. We were created with His love. We are made from His love. Our deepest and most wondrous feelings deep in our soul must reach up and return that love to God in kind.

He has given us His love as a gift, a gift we can share with others, and a gift we can give back to Him, as well. Love is the only thing that multiplies immeasurably when shared.

Our prayers must be founded in love and pure in their intentions. God will never grant a request to harm another one of His children or inflict pain on one of them. He will never honor an evil desire or petition of hate. These things are not the ways of prayer. Petitions of this kind are not prayers at all.

Love does no harm to its neighbor. Therefore love is the fulfillment of the law. Romans 13:10

More About Prayer

Prayer can be formal or informal, much like any other conversation you have with someone you love and respect. If something is on your mind, you can talk to God about it. He knows your thoughts, your fears and worries, the desires of your heart. He even knows all the bad things you've done in your life, and He loves you anyway. No matter what is on your mind, you can take it to Him in prayer.

Prayer is simply a conversation with God about anything that comes to mind. Only unlike human beings, God is always there for you—no matter where you are, what time of day it is, or what is going on in your life. He won't desert you or get too busy for you. He will never leave you alone or abandon you. Many times throughout the Bible God tells us this.

In the Old Testament He told Moses: *"The Lord himself goes before you and will be with you; he will never leave you nor forsake you. Do not be afraid; do not be discouraged."* Deuteronomy 31:8

And later He told Joshua: *"...As I was with Moses, so I will be with you; I will never leave you nor forsake you."* Joshua 1:5

And again in Hebrews 13:5 we read *...because God has said, "Never will I leave you; never will I forsake you."*

We have His blessed assurance that we are never truly alone. He is always with us, even to the very end of the world. *"...And surely I am with you always, to the very end of the age."* Matthew 28:20

When you feel scared or alone, you can call on Him. When you are worried or upset, He is there. When you are happy and overjoyed, He is there, too.

Unfortunately, many of us tend to forget about Him when the going is good and remember to call on Him only when things are difficult. Despite this, He is still readily available for us when we do call on Him and never turns His back on us in retaliation.

How many of our friends on earth could be so kind and forgiving? I doubt we could be that kind and forgiving ourselves. What kind of person would you be if you only called on your friends when you were nervous or in trouble, when you needed or wanted something, or felt lonely and scared? That's how we often treat God. Yet He always welcomes us back with open arms.

God's power and compassion are awesome and almost unimaginable. To think that His one and only Son died to save us from our sins is almost unthinkable. But to know that it is so is to be reassured that God loves us so incredibly much, more than anything comprehensible here on earth.

- ✟ Are you sometimes at a loss for words when you try to pray?
- ✟ Do you worry that you're not saying the "right" things when you pray?
- ✟ Do you sometimes feel like you don't know *how* to pray properly?
- ✟ Do you sometimes feel unworthy of God's time and attention?
- ✟ Is it sometimes hard to talk to God? To tell Him what's really on your mind?
- ✟ Do you ever feel undeserving of His love or blessings in your life?
- ✟ Do you ever feel selfish for praying to Him, asking Him for help, or taking up His valuable time?

Pray With Me...

Dear Lord,
Help me to remember that it is never too late to start a personal relationship with you.

I know I haven't always done the right things or been the best person. I've made a lot of mistakes, and I am not deserving of your love and forgiveness, but you offer it freely to me anyway.

Help me to accept your gifts and to come to you in prayer with an honest and sincere heart.

Help my faith to grow.
I place my hope in you.
I love you, Lord.
Amen

Chapter 4: The Power of Prayer

He Has the Power

I can do everything through him who gives me strength. Philippians 4:13

Commit to the Lord whatever you do, and your plans will succeed. Proverbs 16:3

Trust in the Lord with all your heart and lean not on your own understanding; in all your ways acknowledge him, and he will make your paths straight. Proverbs 3:5-6

I pray also that the eyes of your heart may be enlightened in order that you may know the hope to which he has called you, the riches of his glorious inheritance in the saints, and his incomparably great power for us who believe... Ephesians 1:18-19

Let Go of Your Limits

Could it be that you have limited your life by your own limited expectations? Maybe somehow you came to believe that you could never have a life of happiness and peace. Maybe someone told you that you would "never be" what you wanted to be or never have the life you wanted to have.

Subconsciously, you may be limiting yourself. And in the process, you may also be limiting the power of God in your life.

Stop limiting God! God is without limits!

Tap into *His* Power

Tap into the awesome and incredible power of God. God created the heavens and the earth and every living thing on our planet in only six days. He spoke it all into being. He simply said, "Let there be..." and it was. We are talking about an immense power greater than anything we can imagine here on earth, and that power is available to us through prayer.

Through prayer, we develop a very special, intimate one-on-one relationship with God. Our lives become more peaceful and we are more confident—not as a result of our own accomplishments, but because we are drawing on the most powerful source in all the world, the one who created us and rules all things. We feel inspired to do things we may not have believed possible before when God whispers His will into our souls.

We can achieve more than we ever thought possible because we are no longer trying to do it all on our own. Now we are in harmony with the one who governs all, and what more could we possibly ask for than His divine intervention?

"Great is our Lord and mighty in power;..." Psalm 147:5

"...with God all things are possible." Matthew 19:26

Don't Second Guess God

When you pray, do you ask God for something specific? Do you limit yourself and therefore God's gift to you by setting parameters on it? Why not pray an open-ended prayer and leave the deciding up to God? You might be very pleasantly surprised to see He has something much greater in store for you than you could ever have imagined!

When you pray, do you tell God how to answer your request? Do you tell Him *how* to do His job? Do you really think He needs you to spell it all out for Him. Do you really care that much about *how* He provides for your needs and desires? Why do we feel the need to control every step of the process? When will we learn that we are not in control—God is?

Quit telling God what to do and how to do it. God is in the results business. When we believe in His awesome power, when we have faith that He can do all things, He will constantly and repeatedly amaze and astonish us with the great things He can do.

When we pray for something, we must put our entire trust and faith in God's power and believe without a doubt that He will deliver on His promises.

The Bible tells us time and time again that God's awesome and incredible power is the key to everything.

When you pray for something, ask for what you desire, believe that you have received it, and begin thanking Him for that blessing just as if you already have it. Thank Him for His wondrous gifts, smile, get excited, and *know* it will come to be. Don't worry about *how* He will provide. Just know that He will.

"If you believe, you will receive whatever you ask for in prayer." Matthew 21:22

God Gets Results

If you ask the Lord for a way to get back and forth to work each day because your car is broken down, what difference does it make *how* He grants your request as long as He does? Don't limit yourself and limit God by placing parameters on your request. He will answer your prayers in whatever way is in accordance with His plan.

Focus on the result you are looking for and pray for that result. Don't worry yourself with the details. In looking at the example of getting back and forth to work each day, think of the countless ways God could choose to grant your request and all the blessings that might result from the way He chooses.

Perhaps He will provide you with the offer of a ride from a friend or co-worker, enabling you to talk with that friend and catch up on each others' lives.

Maybe He arranges for a neighbor to give you a lift and in the course of your daily drives you learn that here is a lonely soul who needed some company and companionship even more than you needed the ride.

You might get a bus pass from a co-worker who will be on vacation and won't be using it and one day have the opportunity to sit next to someone who really needed to hear about the Jesus you know and love when she was having an awful day—something, anything that would give her the hope to go on.

Maybe your car will be repaired in time for the week or it will be found to be beyond repair and you will trade it in at just the right time and get a great deal on the used car of your dreams that just came onto the lot.

God will find the way. When you pray, focus on the results and the outcomes and let Him handle the details. As Richard Carlson's books suggest, "Don't sweat the small stuff." Leave the details to Him.

And we know that in all things God works for the good of those who love him, who have been called according to his purpose. Romans 8:28

He Knows What He's Doing

Prayer is power, but not the kind of power we human beings normally think of. Through God's power in prayer, we cannot "make" other people or things obey our command. We cannot call upon God to give us everything we desire on a whim. But praying to God and thereby tapping into His power, when done with humble and sincere faith in God, can bring about miraculous things.

If it is God's will, prayer can change people, attitudes, and circumstances. By praying and calling upon God to provide for our needs, we affirm to Him that we want His blessings in our life. We open the door for Him to perform miracles for us.

The remarkable power of prayer has resulted in many phenomena that cannot otherwise be explained—the miraculous healing of a terminally ill person, sparing a life in circumstances when a person should have been killed, and the birth of a child to people thought to be infertile, for example. Many people readily acknowledge such things as miracles because they cannot be scientifically or medically explained. God's power is great and in such circumstances He shows us the depth of His power.

Smaller miracles happen everyday, all around us, and frequently go unnoticed. Though they may not be recognized as such, God's awesome power is at work in our lives when we pray—keeping us safe, helping us avoid that car accident, when the check arrives just in time to pay the rent, or when a friend calls at just the right time, when we needed someone to talk to.

It is impossible to measure the power of prayer and for nonbelievers very difficult to prove that this power even exists. Still, I have seen this power at work and I've been witness to miracles, large and small, that came to pass through the prayers of believers.

When we pray, we develop a strong confidence, a deep internal knowing that all *is* right with our world and will work to our good because God has a plan, even if we don't understand what it is from moment to moment.

We know that He knows what He's doing and that is enough. And considering He created the heavens and the earth and all that is in only six days, *shouldn't* that be enough?

God blesses us daily in a thousand little ways. His love and assurance makes it possible for us to live our lives in service to Him, to do what we know is right and true even when it is difficult in a secular world, and to give our all to everything we do. We no longer need concern ourselves with the daily problems and trivial worries of the day because we know He has it all under control. We can proceed in confidence and assurance that when we follow His will, we will be cared for and protected along the way.

Our paths will be made straight, as the Bible says. We will have guidance, and He will control those things which we cannot, and we have the blessed assurance that even though we do not know what is around each bend in our road, He does, and He will give us the strength to deal with it, no matter what it is.

Believe In His Guidance

I affirm this belief and faith in a short prayer I pray daily, adopted from a prayer in one of Norman Vincent Peale's books:

I believe I am divinely guided.

I believe I will always be led to take the right turn in the road.

I believe God will make a way where there is no way.

Perhaps this prayer or an adaptation of it will help you in your life. I know it has strengthened and sustained me and given me confidence and hope in mine.

Learning to Believe

Part of the inherent power in prayer is knowing and believing without a doubt that God can and does answer all our prayers.

"If you believe, you will receive whatever you ask for in prayer." Matthew 21:22

Because we are human, this can be very difficult sometimes. It is easy to doubt. There are a few techniques you can utilize in your prayer life to increase your faith and enhance your prayers.

1. Plant a Tiny Seed of Faith

Start out with the seed of faith you have, even if you still harbor some doubts. Plant it in your heart, nurture it, and watch it grow.

"I tell you the truth, if you have faith as small as a mustard seed, you can say to this mountain, 'Move from here to there' and it will move. Nothing will be impossible for you." Matthew 17:20

2. Focus on the Positive

Always focus on the positive in prayer. If you truly take an objective look at your life, you will realize the blessings you have received far outweigh the difficulties you've endured. As in all things, sometimes it's just a matter of looking at the glass as half full instead of half empty. Which do you choose? It is a choice, you know—a conscious decision you make, each and every day.

Remember: you attract that which you focus on. If you focus on negatives, you will attract negatives. If you focus on positives, you will attract positives.

We often have a hand in creating our own reality based on what we choose to focus on. If we direct our energies and prayers toward a negative result, is it any wonder that we feel negative and downtrodden? Yet if we think positive thoughts and concentrate on goodness and light, how can we not feel uplifted and renewed?

Our perception is our reality. We see what we think we see. We become what we believe we can become. There is great power in positive thinking and a great deal of proof that our thinking affects our actions and our outcomes. It is the age-old idea that we become a self-fulfilling prophecy.

So focus on the positive and bring your energy to the Lord to be used in His glory.

3. Visualize it and Affirm it

When you pray, visualize and affirm your prayers are working. See your prayers being answered in your mind's eye. Visualize your prayers being answered positively and the Lord granting your request. Think through the details and clearly and really "see" it.

Use daily affirmations that God *is* answering your prayers. It may help to write your affirmations down on paper and read them aloud to yourself each morning and even several times during the day.

Affirmations should be written in a positive statement *"as if"* your request has already been granted but ending with "or something better." Always leave the door open to God's will and the opportunity for Him to bless you beyond your wildest dreams with even more than you dared to hope or pray for.

If you've never used affirmations before, let me explain how this works. An affirmation is a positive statement that, if closely held, believed in, and focused on, can and will come true. It is in many ways just like a prayer, only instead of being worded as a request as many prayers are, it is worded positively "as if" it has already come to pass.

Of course, this is the very essence of how Jesus teaches us to pray—with complete faith and confidence that our prayers are already being answered.

Using affirmations and prayers together is a wonderful, powerful combination.

In your affirmations, as in your prayers, it is important to focus on positive things you want to see happen in your life, but it is even more important that you leave the door open to *God's* will for your life—and the potential for even better results.

Here's an example for you: "I am happily receiving emails and letters from women who used *When A Woman Prays* as a catalyst to help them develop a close, personal, intimate relationship with God or something even better."

Affirmations are a wonderful tool to use in all areas of your life and as a self-help/development tool. They are even more uplifting and powerful when used in combination with your prayers.

The example I shared contains several important elements of an effective affirmation. It tells how I will *feel* when God answers my prayers. It states it *as if* God has already answered my prayer even though since at this moment I am obviously still writing the book, this hasn't physically occurred. It also assumes several outcomes that I fervently hope will result, in this case, that women will read my book and it will touch them in a way that helps them grow closer to God, that they will respond positively to the book's message, and that obviously it will sell enough copies to reach out and make a difference.

It also leaves the door wide open for God to answer my prayer in an even better or more wonderful way as he sees fit, perhaps even in ways that are in or beyond my wildest dreams—such as getting my book featured on *Oprah* or becoming a featured selection in the Crossings bookclub or being sold on QVC!

4. Count Your Blessings

Pray with thanksgiving to God for all the blessings you've been given, not with anger or frustration over the trials and difficulties you've had to endure. In other words, focus on the positive in all circumstances.

Some of the difficulties you've experienced are simply a part of being human—unavoidable things we all have to go through at one time or another. Other misfortunes we bring upon ourselves when we make poor choices. And a few of our perceived troubles may be lessons God is giving us to learn or blessings in disguise. But the important thing to remember is *all* people will have troubles and difficulties. It's normal, and you're no exception. So accept it and don't focus on it.

Instead, make a conscious effort to dwell on the blessings you have received and to praise God for His goodness to you. It may be helpful to create a gratitude journal where you list things you are thankful for each day. This can help heighten your awareness of all the ways you are blessed in your life. Give thanks to God for all your blessings and the abundance in your life. Consider little blessings like a soft, warm bed and a bright, sunny day as well as the bigger things you usually focus on like a good job and healthy children.

God's Power is Beyond Comprehension

It's easy to think you shouldn't bother God with the little stuff—you know, trivial things. God is so magnificent, important, and busy—and He has big, important things to take care of and important prayers to hear. Certainly there are people in the world who need His help with a lot of big, critical things—people who have lost their homes or jobs, people who grieve for a loved one, people who have just been diagnosed with a serious illness and need healing. Who are we to take up His valuable time with frivolous requests?

Think about the immensity of God's job already. Can you imagine communicating with and hearing prayers from and watching over billions of people on earth all at the same time? It is beyond our human comprehension. But God's power *is* beyond comprehension. He is the most awesome, powerful force that has ever existed. He can do anything.

God Has No Limits

By telling ourselves that God won't have time for our requests, we are limiting God. But God is limitless. His power is without boundaries.

We are used to looking at things from a human perspective. But God is not human.

"...With man this is impossible, but with God all things are possible." Matthew 19:26

Just as God can be available to each and every one of us every minute of every day, He can also be available to us for the little things as well as the big crisis situations. And in fact, He wants to be. He wants to be a part of everything and all aspects of our lives. He wants us to come to Him with all our concerns—big and small. He wants to be our very best friend, and He will always be there for us.

An Answered Prayer

No problem is too big or too small for God. As I grew up, somehow I got the idea that God was only there to handle the "big" problems—the ones too tough for me to handle on my own. I thought it was my responsibility to try to deal with things myself, but if I absolutely couldn't do it or cope with it alone, I could call on Him for reinforcements. I thought with all the millions of people on earth, God would not have time for my little requests or small problems. He was too busy to be bothered with trivial concerns.

As an adult, I read somewhere that God wants to be involved in *all* aspects of our life. He wants to be our trusted friend, our confidante. He wants to have an ongoing relationship with us. He wants to communicate with us every day, all day long even. We should talk to Him throughout the day, as we go about our daily lives. He is never too busy for us. Even with all the people on this earth, He can give each and every one of us His undivided attention. What a miracle! It's beyond our human comprehension.

But I know it's true. I cannot count all the times in my adult life that He has helped with simple little requests. All I've had to do is ask…

One of my hobbies is cross-stitching, and some years ago I discovered there weren't all that many cross-stitch kits or designs that were Christian in nature. And I thought this might be a nice little market niche for me. So I started to design my own.

One of my first projects featured a simple birdhouse with vines of ivy forming a border around the piece. And below the birdhouse I wanted to stitch a Biblical saying about birds, specifically sparrows.

Now I knew there were passages in the Bible about sparrows, because I had heard our pastor quote some of them in church and he even sang a song about a sparrow in weeks or months prior. But I didn't know where to find these kinds of passages in the Bible.

You see, when I grew up, no emphasis was placed on memorizing scripture. My faith at that time emphasized memorization of specific prayers. So I was new to reading the Bible and I didn't know where to look.

But I took out the Bible anyway, and I explained the situation to God. I said, "You know I'm creating these cross-stitch designs to honor you. And you know I have this birdhouse here and these nice little ivy leaves, and I was thinking a scripture passage would make it complete. I'm envisioning something about sparrows. Now I know there are Bible passages about sparrows, but I have no idea where to look. Will you help me?"

And so I opened the Bible and put my finger down on a random page and began to read. And there on that very same page, I found the following passage:

> *Even the sparrow has found a home,*
> *and the swallow a nest for herself,*
> *a place near your altar,*
> *O Lord Almighty,*
> *my King and my God.*
> *Blessed are those who dwell in your house;*
> *they are ever praising you.*
> Psalm 84:3-4

Blessings Big and Small

There is no problem too large for our Lord. Our God is an awesome God with a mighty power. Likewise, there is no concern of ours that is too small for His attention. If it weighs on your mind, take it to Him in prayer.

God wants to be involved in every area of our lives.

- ✞ Have you ever had a problem you just couldn't deal with on your own?
- ✞ Are you often overwhelmed by everything you have to deal with on a daily basis and have trouble fitting it all in?
- ✞ Do you feel fearful or uneasy?
- ✞ Do you sometimes get yourself "in over your head" and wish someone would bail you out?
- ✞ Do you sometimes feel weak or helpless against the world?

Pray With Me...

Dear Lord,
Sometimes I think I can take on the world all by myself. All too soon it falls apart and I am reminded that I am only one person. I cannot do it all, and even what I do accomplish is not always as good as I wanted it to be.

During times like these I realize that I don't *have* to do it all on my own. I don't have to carry my burdens alone. You are with me always and your awesome power is more powerful than other power that exists. If it is your will, you can overcome anything!

All I need to do is remember to include you in my daily life and to call upon you and your mighty power through my prayers, and you are right there by my side.

Thank you, Lord, for being so close to me and blessing me time and time again.

Amen

Chapter 5: Formal Prayer

Early Memories

The very first prayer I remember learning as a child was called the Guardian Angel prayer. It went like this:

> Angel of God, my guardian dear
> To whom God's love commits me near
> Ever this day be at my side
> To light and guard, to rule and guide.
> Amen

As a child, I was instructed in my Christian faith and over the years, I learned many formal prayers. I memorized these prayers and could recite them or pray them whenever I liked. Some of them were used during our Sunday worship services, others I said at bedtime, and some were traditional before and after meal prayers. I call these "formal" prayers because I believe prayer can take several different forms and the memorization of a written prayer seems to be one of the more formal approaches.

Ritual and Tradition

As a child and for many years, these formal, memorized prayers served me very well. In reciting these prayers, I learned to begin communicating with God at a young age. I learned of His existence, learned that I could talk with Him, and began to develop my faith. These prayers were the traditional way I saw my parents and relatives communicating with God. It was one of the ways we demonstrated our belief and lived our faith.

The familiarity of the prayers became somewhat of a ritual and a comfort. They were part of a long-standing tradition, and it gave me a feeling of belonging to a large community of believers all across the world and stretching back through history. This connection was important to me.

A Way to Begin

For some of you, formal prayer may be a way to begin. You may wish to select several prayers that are meaningful to you personally, communicate what you would like to say to God, and "get you talking" to Him, so to speak. You can use formal prayers that are meaningful to you and the practice of your faith or formal prayers that simply strike a chord within you and "feel right." At the end of this book, you will also find prayers I have written and prayed for reasons that were particularly important to me. You can certainly feel free to use any of them in your own prayer life or to customize them for your circumstances. You may even want to write your own.

If you feel at a loss for words, formal or written prayers can help you get started.

The Webster's dictionary definition of prayer that corresponds with the Christian faith goes something like this:

prayer – 1. the act or practice of praying, as to God; 2. an earnest request; entreaty; or supplication; 3. a) a humble and sincere request to God; b) an utterance to God in praise, thanksgiving, confession, etc.; c) any set formula for praying to God; 4. in some religions, a devotional service consisting chiefly of prayers; 5. any spiritual communion with God; or 6. something prayed for or requested, as in a petition

"Communion" in this sense is described as:

communion – the act of sharing one's thoughts and emotions with another or others; intimate converse; an intimate relationship with deep understanding

As you can see, prayer has several definitions, and it may mean different things to different people. From my perspective, prayer can be all of these things and so much more. I define prayer very simply as "the act of sharing one's thoughts and emotions with God." It is the act of communicating with God.

I believe this act of praying and sharing can take many forms. Each person must choose the most meaningful and effective method for them personally. That may be formal prayer or less formal or alternate forms of prayer. One form is no better than another, but for some of us, some forms will be more comfortable than others. It is also common for people to pray in more than one way and for their preferred method of prayer to change over time.

The Perfect Prayer

If you are struggling and don't know quite where to start, I would like to suggest you begin with a formal, written prayer that is quite possibly the most perfect prayer ever written. It comes from the words Jesus spoke in Matthew 6:9-13. This is the version I learned. It is called *The Lord's Prayer*. Some denominations also refer to it as the *Our Father*.

The Lord's Prayer

Our Father who art in heaven
Hallowed be thy name
Thy kingdom come
Thy will be done
On earth as it is in heaven.
Give us this day our daily bread
And forgive us our trespasses,
As we forgive those who trespass against us
And lead us not into temptation
But deliver us from evil.
Amen

All through my life, this prayer has had a calming, soothing effect on my soul and the ruffled feathers of my earthly existence. When things are going wrong or I am deeply troubled, it often helps to reflect on this and other familiar prayers. Because they are committed to memory, they come easily to mind when I am sometimes at a loss for words of my own.

Jesus Teaches us to Pray

Why does *The Lord's Prayer* uplift me and why do I call it the most perfect prayer? Jesus, Himself, tells us to pray using the words of *The Lord's Prayer.* His wisdom captures every element of perfect prayer.

The first line reads: "Our Father who art in heaven." It acknowledges God as our heavenly father and calls on Him, as all prayers do.

"Hallowed be thy name" is another way of saying that God's very name is blessed and holy. As our creator and Lord of all, we are honoring Him and giving Him the respect, love, and admiration He so richly deserves.

"Thy kingdom come" acknowledges that we are a creation in God's world—in God's kingdom. He is the ruler over all.

"Thy will be done, On earth as it is in heaven" tells God that we know He has the master plan. We acknowledge here that God's will is supreme and even though we may petition Him according to our needs and desires, we recognize and choose to follow not our own will, but His will for our lives. We are ready, willing, and able to follow His calling, whatever that may be. Just as the angels in heaven take their direction from Him, so will we.

When we say "Give us this day our daily bread," we are asking God to provide for our needs today. We are not asking for tomorrow or the next day or the year after that. We are simply, each and every day, asking Him that He take care of us just as He promised us He would.

"And forgive us our trespasses, As we forgive those who trespass against us." Here we admit that we are sinners and ask God to forgive us our sins and our sinful nature. At the same time we acknowledge that we, too, must forgive those who have sinned against us. For how can we expect or accept forgiveness from God for our own indiscretions if we cannot likewise give and share that gift of forgiveness with others. God calls us to extend the hand and love of forgiveness to others just as He has forgiven us.

Over and over again He has forgiven us our sins, and we are called to forgive others likewise.

Then Peter came to Jesus and asked, "Lord, how many times shall I forgive my brother when he sins against me? Up to seven times?"

Jesus answered, "I tell you not seven times, but seventy-seven times." Mathew 18:21-22

When we say "And lead us not into temptation, But deliver us from evil," we ask God to keep us out of harm's way, to keep us from those things or circumstances that will tempt us, and to surround us with His grace so that Satan cannot get near us to do damage. Rather than be faced with opportunities to sin, we ask God to help us steer clear of those pitfalls knowing full well that being surrounded by temptation and evils makes it even harder to be true to God.

We are only human and it is much easier for us if God can help keep us away from temptation in the first place, but if we find ourselves among evil, we ask Him to help us out of that situation.

Some versions of *The Lord's Prayer* end with the sentence, "For thine is the kingdom, and the power, and the glory, now and forever," summarizing God's identity and His power and authority over all.

Uniting Christians

Most Christian churches incorporate reciting *The Lord's Prayer* into each of their church services. Repeating the comforting and familiar words week after week, year after year, *The Lord's Prayer* helps unite Christians everywhere in a common belief and purpose—focusing on the essence of God's love rather than the specific factors that divide Christianity into various denominations.

The 23rd Psalm

Another well-known prayer is taken from Scripture and is often used as a source of comfort, particularly during very difficult times in our lives or when a loved one is seriously ill. This prayer, taken from and known as *The 23rd Psalm* also brings comfort when someone we love dies and we are grieving because we know that we are never alone, even in what may seem like our darkest hours.

Psalm 23*

The Lord is my shepherd; I shall not want.
He maketh me to lie down in green pastures: he leadeth me beside the still waters.
He restoreth my soul: he leadeth me in the paths of righteousness for his name's sake.
Yea, though I walk through the valley of the shadow of death, I will fear no evil: for thou art with me; thy rod and thy staff they comfort me.
Thou preparest a table before me in the presence of mine enemies: thou annointest my head with oil; my cup runneth over.
Surely goodness and mercy shall follow me all the days of my life: and I will dwell in the house of the Lord for ever.

Even the language of *The 23rd Psalm* is beautiful and reassuring.

Formal, memorized prayers like this—those we know "by heart" can be such a wonderful comfort to us when we are troubled. They can strengthen our faith and understanding immeasurably, and I would encourage everyone to commit prayers or special Biblical passages to memory. It is just one of several meaningful and inspirational ways to pray.

*Note: For this Scripture, I elected to quote from the King James Version of the Holy Bible, as that is the eloquent verse I heard most often growing up and learned to love.

Teaching Our Children to Pray

As a woman and mother, it is our joy, duty, and responsibility to teach our children to pray. We can begin by praying for them and over them at the very beginning of their lives. We can even pray for our babies before they are born.

As our children grow and we teach them about their faith, Bible stories and formal prayers are especially helpful in explaining somewhat abstract concepts. Formal, memorized prayers help children learn to communicate with God early in their lives in a way that is easy and simple to understand. In introducing our children to prayer when they are small, we open the lines of communication between God and our children so they will grow up knowing He is always there for them and He is just a whisper or a thought away.

- ♱ Do you remember the first prayer you ever learned?
- ♱ Do memorized prayers bring you comfort during times of distress?
- ♱ Are formal prayers a welcome way to communicate with God and honor Him when you are at a loss for words?
- ♱ How are you teaching your children to know God?
- ♱ What prayers do your children know?

Pray With Me...

Dear Lord,
When I am at a loss for words or my troubles seem too deep to express in my own words, I feel so blessed to have the words that Jesus taught us to pray to you and open the lines of communication between us.

The words of some of the Psalms and other passages in Scripture are a comfort to me. The ritual and tradition of formal prayer is a familiar blessing to me.

Thank you for providing me with loving parents, friends, and teachers who, like Jesus, taught me how to pray to you.

Amen

Chapter 6:
Not So Formal Prayer

Prayer is More Than Just Words

There is no "right" way to pray. There are no magic words. A child can pray. A professor with a Phd. can pray. It isn't *necessary* to memorize words or Scripture, though you can if that is helpful and meaningful to you, as we discussed in the last chapter. But to God, it doesn't make any difference how eloquent your words sound.

It Begins in the Heart and Soul

What is important to God is the sincerity behind the prayer. It's what's in your heart and soul that counts.
    Simply speak to God from your heart. At times, this may be in the form of silent prayer. Sometimes you will find yourself shouting and other times whispering. Your prayer make take the form of song—singing and dancing in praise. Or a quiet stillness, like meditation, simply concentrating on God's presence in your life and the peace it brings to you.

A Personal Choice

No one form of prayer is better than another. You will need to do what is comfortable for you. Prayer is—and is meant to be—a very personal thing. It is a part of your very own special relationship with God.

If you are comfortable praying out loud and sharing your prayers with others, do so. If you are not, then talk to God in your own time and your own way. Speak to Him in the quiet and calm—in church or at home, while you are walking or sitting or driving, before you go to sleep at night at the close of your day, and upon waking in the morning to begin a new day. You can even pray in the bathtub, remember?

Communicate with Him at all times—through word and song, in thought and deed, in the example you set for others.

As a child, I learned many formal prayers and committed them to memory.

Today I often use a more spontaneous form of prayer than I did as a child, and I've tried to share that with my children, as well. I don't need formal prayers or words to communicate with God, though I sometimes use them. More often, though, I use my own words and talk to Him as if I am talking to a friend.

Often the children and I take turns praying out loud in the car on the way to school. This is a great way to introduce your children to what living your faith means to you—by letting them see some of your imperfections and worries and how you turn to God in your daily life for guidance. It also lets them hear you praise Him firsthand for the blessings He has provided and encourages them to do the same. Finally, it is an opportunity to get to know your children and what is on their minds. It is a meaningful time shared with your children and your Lord and it helps your children learn how to develop their own personal relationship with God.

If you are not yet comfortable praying out loud, that is OK, too. Remember, each of you must develop a prayer life that is comfortable to you. When you get comfortable with it, then you can share it with others if you desire.

Sing, Praise, and Worship

One of my favorite ways to pray, praise, and worship God is through song. I love to sing His praises. To me it is one of the ultimate spiritual experiences and it fills me with complete joy to sing to Him and for Him. My entire body, soul, and spirit join in worshiping God when I lift my voice to Him in songs of praise.

It is the one and only time I can sing without feeling overly self-conscious because that singing glorifies my Father in heaven and helps convey the depth of my love and honor for Him. In the midst of a Christian song, my body moves in rhythm to the music, my eyes will close, and I can feel God's presence near me. It is, at least momentarily, as if I have stepped out of my normal, human life to be with the Lord completely.

Some would argue that singing is not praying. However, I believe that singing is one more way of praying that should not be overlooked. Singing involves the entire body and spirit. It can be moving, inspiring, and uplifting. Always it is expressive in a way that surpasses words alone. In the midst of a beautiful spiritual song, the music and the experience can "take over" in a way many traditional prayers can't.

Love, joy, and thanksgiving flow out from our hearts and souls in communion with God and carry our deepest feelings with the music. It is a wonderful and complete feeling one must experience to appreciate.

Prayer Moves Emotions

Jesus is so happy when we lift our voices to praise and worship Him–whether in words or in song or with our music. He loves to listen to the joy in our voices because it flows from our hearts and souls straight up to heaven.

Sometimes when I sing or pray, I have been known to cry. The moment with my Lord becomes so intense and real that my eyes fill with tears. It may be an overwhelming feeling of peace or joy. Sometimes it is just that my heart is filled to overflowing and ready to burst from the unconditional love and acceptance I feel Him sending to me. It wraps around me like a warm blanket, enveloping me with a feeling it is difficult to explain, and I know this is just a glimpse of what heaven will be like.

The moment and the feelings are so intense, so joyful, and so complete. It is the moment we are living for. I feel safe, secure, protected, loved, and cherished. My worries are put to rest, and I often feel close to the loved ones who have gone before me because I know they are with Him experiencing this same overwhelming love.

I feel complete, whole, calm, and yet emotionally so full that I cannot contain the feeling. It spills over and I have to share it with someone else. I have to love someone else. I have to tell them about this Jesus that loves me so much. I want to reach out and hug someone tight, to rejoice in this love I have found, to share it with others and bring them into the loving embrace He has me in.

Write God a Letter

Another less traditional means of praying is to write a letter to God. Some people have a hard time focusing or organizing their thoughts. For them it may be easier to put things in writing than to verbalize them.

Writing a letter to God or writing your innermost thoughts and prayers in a journal is an excellent way to pray in silence, clarify your thoughts and desires, and communicate them with God.

Writing your thoughts and prayers down also provides you with a wonderful record of your prayers and communication with Him, and it is a heartwarming experience to go back to your journal or letters after a few weeks, a month, or even a year and to re-read those prayers, noting how every single one was answered—even if it isn't always the way we had expected.

If you are prone to doubting God or the miraculous power of prayer, I encourage you to keep a prayer journal and to do just that. You will be amazed and uplifted to see the power of prayer at work in your life.

- ☦ How do you feel when you sing songs of praise to God?
- ☦ Do you ever feel closer to God outside, in a natural setting, than in a church?
- ☦ Do you sometimes feel like you are praying to God when you just sit and "be" with him in silence?
- ☦ What are you doing when you feel closest to God?
- ☦ How do you celebrate your love for the Lord?

Pray With Me...

Dear Lord,
Everything I do is a celebration of my love for you. Every way that I communicate with you builds on our relationship and becomes the essence of prayer. Sometimes it is with words or music. Sometimes it is in silence or a deep sigh. I can speak the words aloud, whisper them to you softly, shout them from the rooftops, or write them down in private—it doesn't matter *how* I do it. You are right there hearing my words, spoken and unspoken, and understanding what is in my heart in a way that I could never put into words.

Thank you for taking the time to get to know me so well and for giving me so many ways to communicate with you.
Amen

Chapter 7: Praying for Others

Making a Difference

Did you know that your prayers can reach out and touch other people's lives, too? Your prayers can bless them even if they don't know you're praying for them and sometimes even if *they* don't believe.

Our prayers can have a remarkable impact on others lives, affecting them in ways you can only imagine. Just as in praying for yourself and your own desires, it is especially important that when you pray for others, you remember to let God's wisdom guide you.

When we pray for others, we should always consciously pray for their higher good and for God's will to be fulfilled in their lives. That can be really hard. Sometimes we are tempted to pray for what *we* want for others rather than what is best for them, under the guise of "praying for them." For instance, praying for someone to do what *we* want them to do based on our motives is often more a selfish request than a sincere prayer.

In other cases, we stubbornly pray asking God to change other people—and that's not really what God or prayer is all about. Through His action in their lives and through their own decisions, yes, people can and often do change, but that should not necessarily be the basis of our prayers for them.

If we sincerely pray for change in our lives, we must be willing to accept that the first changes God chooses to make may be in *us*, and we must be willing to accept those changes in ourselves rather than trying to change someone else.

So who should you pray for? In a word, everyone. But more specifically, let's start with those people who are closest to you—those people you love the most. You will be blessed to see how all of your relationships improve when you pray for your loved ones.

Pray for your husband, your children, your family, and your friends with God's highest intent for them in mind. Pray that God will guide them daily, show them His will and make their hearts open to receiving Him, and that He will use you as an instrument to help reach out to them on His behalf. Pray that they will follow His will and accept His gift of love and forgiveness and one day enjoy eternal life in heaven with Him. This is the greatest blessing you could ever ask for anyone you love.

Pray that He will bless them and keep them, and commit them into His loving care.

Praying For Your Husband

If you are married and were married in the Christian church, you know that God intended for you and your husband to become as one flesh when you took your vows. It even says so right in the Bible. And if you are married, you also know that *that* is much easier said than done.

Despite your love for each other and all your best intentions, you are two people with two individual minds and wills of your own. That can make for some interesting "conversations" when you each have a different outlook on things. You're bound to disagree and even argue and squabble like children at times. You will not always see eye to eye, and in fact, you are not meant to. God created each of you the way you are with a special purpose in mind. Both of your viewpoints are valuable.

In the heat of the moment, however, it can be hard to remember that. You may not be thinking rationally or you may not even care about your husband's viewpoint at the time. Sometimes we simply want our own way.

Sometimes it is the other way around. Even if we know we are right, our husbands may disagree. Harsh words fly from our mouths, feelings get hurt, and our relationship can be damaged.

But when we married, not only did we become one with our husband—God entered into our union, as well. Despite the hurting, God can bring healing into our relationships. You can invite Him in to work His healing power in your marriage through your prayers—prayers for your husband and your marriage.

Probably the first obstacle to overcome in praying for our husbands is our temptation to pray that God will change *him* into the person we think we want him to be. The plain and simple fact is that we cannot change another person and even our most fervent prayers may not change our husbands unless they are open to changing. The other—sometimes harder to swallow fact—is that often our prayers will be answered in ways we do not expect.

Maybe *we* are the ones who need to do some changing. Perhaps by changing the way we handle certain situations or react to things, our husbands will have the opportunity for positive change. That can be hard medicine to swallow when we think we are in the right or if we let ourselves feel superior to our husbands because *we* are the ones praying for *them*. Lest we begin to feel this way, we must always consciously remind ourselves that we are praying for God's will in our husband's life—not ours. We must pray that God will guide our husband in his thoughts, words, and actions, just as we pray for Him to guide ours. When God is working with both partners in a marriage, real healing can begin.

For marriages that aren't in any kind of serious trouble, praying for your husband and your marriage is powerful preventive medicine for problems and a wonderful way to demonstrate your love for him. God becomes the glue that holds you together from the start.

Pray for your husband's health and safety, pray for him to find fulfillment in his job, with his family, and in his life, and pray for him to find the peace and contentment each of us longs for.

Pray that God will make your marriage strong and bind you together during difficulties instead of pulling you apart. Pray that you will be sensitive to your husband's needs and he, in turn, to yours. Pray that your husband will not be pulled away from you by any of the distractions or temptations of the outside world—whether that be his work, other women, outside interests, or anything else that could come between you. Pray that God will always be a part of your marriage and continue to help your marriage grow stronger each day.

Praying For Your Children

As a mother, there is probably no single more worthwhile and effective thing you can do for your children than to pray for them. It is important to teach them to pray and bring them up in the Christian faith. It is prudent to teach them right from wrong, to discipline them, and to set a good example for them.

But sooner or later, you will be forced to realize that, though your child may have been born of you or raised by you, that child is *not* an extension of you. Children are born with their own, individual free will. One of your jobs as a parent, and often the most difficult, is to let your children go.

Just as God our Father gave *us* free will and the freedom to make our own choices, so He also gave this free will to our children. There will come a time when we have done our best to raise our kids and we need to stand back and see how they do on their own. It can be really hard to watch our children make mistakes, difficult choices, and to stumble and fall.

But it is helpful for us to remember that they are never *really* alone. God is with them every step of the way—watching over them just as He did for you all these years. Pray for God's guidance and direction in your children's lives.

Pray for their health and safety, their goals and desires, their hopes and dreams. Pray that your children will find friends and companions who will be a good and Godly influence in their lives. Pray that their faith will sustain them during difficulties and that they will come to know and love God personally. Pray that their lives will be blessed, and pray for God's will to be fulfilled through them.

Praying For Your Friends and Family

In the same way, pray for your friends and family. Pray for them in a general sense and also ask God for His blessed intervention if you see one of them in need of His special touch.

Perhaps a friend or family member is hanging out with the wrong crowd, going through a divorce, has a sick child, or just lost their job. Maybe a friend has fallen into depression, been diagnosed with cancer, or is simply struggling with some important decisions.

No matter how big or how small their needs, take them to God in prayer. You can tell your friends and family you are praying for them if you wish. It often gives them a great deal of comfort. But you don't need to. You can take your concerns for anyone you care about straight from your heart to God's ears just as you share all of your concerns in all areas of your life with Him in prayer.

You can even pray for unbelievers. Pray that God will show them the truth. Pray that He will use their difficulties to bring them closer to Him. If you think it will offend someone to tell them you are praying for them, then don't. Just pray anyway.

Some of your friends and family will tell you when they are going through a particular challenge or difficulty. They may ask you to pray for them. It is a wonderful thing to be entrusted with such an assignment and one you should not take lightly. Prayer can work miracles. What a gift to be invited to be a part of that.

Likewise, feel free to ask your friends and family to pray for you when you need extra strength and guidance.

Praying For Strangers/Praying With Others

It is even possible and desirable to pray for total strangers—people you see on the street, people you hear about in the news, and people you have never seen or met.

My children attend a parochial school, and their teachers taught them that whenever they hear a siren, they should stop momentarily to bow their heads and pray for whoever is in need. They don't know why the siren in sounding or who is being affected, but we've all come to know that the sound of a siren usually means something is wrong. It is very seldom a noise associated with any good news. More often it indicates a fire, a police call, or an ambulance, and when we hear it in the distance, we know that someone, somewhere needs our prayers. And although we do not know who the person is at that time, we can ask God for His blessing on them without knowing all the details.

The prayer of just one faithful woman can make a difference in the life of a stranger...or a friend...whoever it turns out to be.

If the prayer of a single woman can impact a life, think of how the prayers of many gathered in God's name can affect our world. We often find special grace and blessings when we pray together with others for a common cause.

Most church families regularly ask the congregation to pray intercessory prayers for the specific needs of church members during their weekly service. Often, the prayers are on behalf of someone who is ill, facing surgery, or grieving. While you may not always know the people who are being named at each service, you can pause a moment to empathize with those people, what they are going through, and say a prayer on their behalf.

Prayer chains and prayer hotlines often utilize the telephone to share prayers for people with specific needs. If someone has a prayer request, they can call to talk about it and request that others pray for them about their specific need or concern. Perhaps they call a hotline just to have someone pray with them.

"Again, I tell you that if two of you on earth agree about anything you ask for, it will be done for you by my Father in heaven. For where two or three come together in my name, there am I with them." Matthew 17:19-20

Some people call prayer hotlines when they are in deep distress and simply don't know how to pray. It is a wonderful thing to be on the receiving end of such a call and to help guide someone to God.

With the advent of the Internet, prayers are now making their way through cyberspace with the speed of light. I regularly pray with people online for their needs and the needs of their friends, family members, or complete strangers who need God's loving presence in their lives. Even 10 years ago, who would have thought people would be praying together online?

In many cases, we will never know the outcome of the prayers we say on behalf of strangers. We simply say our prayers and leave it in God's hands in faith that He will provide. In other situations, we are blessed to see the results of people praying all across the world for a common cause—and some of those prayers have resulted in miracles. I've seen it happen: the woman whose cancer went into remission when her husband initiated an all-out prayer campaign on her behalf, successful job interviews for people in dire financial situations who asked for intercessory prayer, and people coming together to share sorrow and grief in the wake of tragedies. Yes, these days God is at work even on the Web. There is nowhere God won't go to share His love.

Praying For Your Enemies

Bless those who persecute you; bless and do not curse...Do not repay anyone evil for evil. Be careful to do what is right in the eyes of everybody. If it is possible, as far as it depends on you, live at peace with everyone. Do not take revenge... Romans 12:14, 17-19

Do not be overcome by evil, but overcome evil with good. Romans 12:21

Get rid of all bitterness, rage and anger, brawling and slander, along with every form of malice. Be kind and compassionate to one another, forgiving each other, just as in Christ God forgave you. Ephesians 4:31-32

"...Love your enemies and pray for those who persecute you..." Matthew 5:44

Pray for your enemies. Boy, this one can be difficult. This is the hardest prayer of all to utter and still harder to say sincerely. Yet God has called us to do just this. We are called to forgive the people who hurt us.

The reasoning behind His call to us makes sense. Resenting people, hostility, anger, and hate can block spiritual power. How can love exist in an atmosphere of hate? Yet God is asking us to take it a step even farther than that. God wants us to be so filled with love—His love—that true forgiveness is really possible.

While it can be very hard to do, try to pray for the people you don't particularly like, people who have mistreated you or been unfair to you, and the people who have hurt you either knowingly or unknowingly. God can help you. He knows how difficult this is for you.

After all, we *are* only human. While Jesus can wash away and forgive our sins, we remember only too well when people have wronged us.

When it's tough to ask for blessings on those who have cursed us, the best way to start is to lay it all out on the line for God, just as we do in every other area of our prayer life. Talk to Him like a friend. Come clean.

Lord, I know I should pray for my enemies and I know I need to find a way to forgive them, but it's just so darn hard! Help me learn to be a forgiving person. Help me learn to see this person and this situation in a different light. Help me let go of my horrible feelings about this. Help me to give and receive your peace and put this in the past.

Remember that God's one and only Son, Jesus, died on the cross for OUR sins and the sins of these people—who are our enemies—too. Though they are our enemies in this moment in time, they, too, are God's children. Jesus died for all of us. If God can forgive us all our awful sins—sins for which His only Son had to die—who are we to withhold forgiveness from another.

Pray for God's wisdom and insight as you struggle through your prayers for your enemies. Ask others to pray for you and with you in this effort.

Pray that God will bless them and build on the goodness within them. Pray that He will change their attitudes and open their hearts to His love. Ask Him to soften your heart toward them and enable you to see them as He sees them.

Despite the difficulty in praying for our enemies, we stand to gain at least as much, if not more benefit, from these prayers. Praying for someone we have every reason to dislike or even hate can free us from those hateful feelings and release them to God's care and ultimate wisdom.

A word of caution here: The people who have hurt you may not ask for your forgiveness. They may not think they need forgiving. They may not think they did anything wrong. They may not even care.

Forgiveness is as much for the peace and well being of *your* soul as it is for the other person. You can forgive someone without telling them. In fact, in some cases the person you need to forgive may no longer be living or easily accessible, and that fact should not prevent you from forgiving them. Their acknowledgement or acceptance of your forgiveness is not necessary for your closure or your peace.

In many cases, it is not even advisable to try to contact the person you have forgiven, as they may not be ready to accept responsibility for any hurt they have caused you and the whole thing could "blow up in your face" or reintroduce the hurt all over again. This act of forgiving people who hurt you is your way of coming to acceptance and peace with God and yourself.

I once heard forgiveness described as "giving up your need or desire to make the other person 'pay' for what they did to you." When we're dealing with human beings, this is as apt a definition as any. Truly, when you forgive someone, you are letting go of the hurt and your need to see this person suffer in some way in retribution for the pain they caused you.

- ✟ Do you pray for your family and friends asking *God's* will, not yours, be done?
- ✟ Do you pray for people you do not know, knowing you will receive nothing this side of heaven in return for your efforts?
- ✟ Can you pray for your enemies or pray that God will help you to do so?
- ✟ Do you pray for forgiveness of your sins and extend that same spirit of forgiveness to others?

Pray With Me...

Dear Lord,
Please bless, keep, and guide the people I love—my husband, my parents and family, my children, my friends. Bless also the people whose lives I touch in any small way and make your presence known in their lives.

And though it is very difficult, particularly if I dwell on the hurt and pain others have caused me in this life, please bless the people who have deliberately or unintentionally inflicted that pain on me and my loved ones. Change their hearts, Lord, and give them a new start, just as you gave me a new start when Jesus died on the cross for me.

Amen

Chapter 8: Finding Forgiveness

Have You Done the Unforgivable?

Some women are so overcome with guilt over their shortcomings and mistakes that they do not believe God could forgive them. They turn away from God and suffer on their own. They are convinced that whatever they have done is so awful that it is beyond forgiveness. But nothing is beyond God's forgiveness.

No matter what you have done—drugs, an abortion, murder, stealing, neglecting your child, lying, committing adultery, cheating—whatever you can think of—none of those things are beyond the scope of God's love and forgiveness.

When we are sincerely sorry for our sins and repent of them, God will wipe away all of those sins and give us a new start.

Embarrassment and shame over sins committed is perfectly normal. In fact, it is a part of feeling and showing remorse for the mistakes we've made, but God does not want you to use these feelings as an excuse to alienate yourself from Him.

When you stay away from God, it hurts Him. He wants to help you. He wants to forgive your sins and welcome you back into His family where you belong. Do you remember the story of the prodigal son? Like the father in that story, God, our Father, is always overjoyed when His children realize their mistakes, turn away from them, and return home to His kingdom.

The important thing is that you learned from your mistakes, right? None of us is without sin and none of us have lived without making errors in judgment or mistakes. But as my mother used to say, "Just because you make one mistake doesn't mean you have to make two."

She used to say this in reference to people who got pregnant outside of marriage and then married "just because" of the pregnancy, not necessarily out of love or for any other valid reason. But the same thing applies here. Yes, you've sinned. You've made mistakes. And maybe some of them are pretty big mistakes at that. But don't make another mistake by turning away from God.

In the midst of your guilt, shame, and pain, Jesus is the only one who can bring you the peace and forgiveness you so desperately need—even if you don't want to admit it to yourself.

Ask For His Forgiveness

Pray to God and ask His forgiveness for your sins. Be honest with Him and be sincere. Tell it like it is and ask for His help. God already knows the truth. He knows what you did and He knows what is on your mind and in your heart. But He wants to hear it from you. It's sort of like when children make mistakes. You already know what they did wrong, but you want them to come to you and honestly tell you what happened. God is our Father, and we are His children. He wants this, too.

God wants you to confess your sins, to repent, and to ask for His forgiveness. His Son paid the ultimate sacrifice that we might share in eternal life with Him in heaven, and God wants everyone to receive the gift of forgiveness. All we have to do is ask.

If we come to Him honestly sorry for our sins, He will forgive us *anything* we have done. Incredible. Unimaginable. God's way.

Forgiving Yourself

Did you know that sometimes it is really harder for us to forgive ourselves than for God to forgive us? It's true. There have been times in my life when I have experienced great remorse for something I've done and I've prayed to God for forgiveness of that sin. I know He forgave me, but I still had a really hard time forgiving myself. In some cases, I couldn't forgive myself until I had apologized to the person I hurt—as painful as it was—and sometimes even when it was years later. But God had really already forgotten all about it. When He forgives our sins, He washes the slate clean. Don't we wish we could forgive *and* forget when someone has hurt us?

Forgiveness is God's Gift

The thing to remember is that we are only human. There are some things that are very hard for human beings to forgive one another for and even to forgive ourselves for. It is sometimes simply beyond our comprehension. But God's way is not our way. He is infinitely more powerful and loving than any human being ever could be. The same power and might that formed the earth and the stars and the sky is the same awesome God that can forgive you your sins no matter how horrible they may seem if you are truly sorry for them. He made it possible for you to be forgiven *anything* when He sacrificed His one and only Son, Jesus, on the cross at Calvary in repentance for our sins.

Can you imagine sacrificing your own child? I can't. It is simply too horrible to grasp. And yet God did it. He did it for us. For you and for me. How could He love us that much?

I don't have an answer for that. It's too hard to comprehend a love so perfect and complete. But He does. He loves us that much.

He loves us more than anyone ever has, ever could, or ever will. His love is perfect and complete and unconditional.

His love brings comfort, peace, and forgiveness when nothing else can. Do not turn away from Him.

Go to Him in sincere sorrow and repentance, and He will forgive you all your sins no matter what they may be.

Moving Forward

No one—except Jesus—ever walked this earth as a perfect person, without sin. Though God will forgive you anything and He calls us to do the same, it can be disappointing and frustrating to remember that most people are far from divine, and as such, they may not forgive or forget so easily.

You will find that even after God has forgiven you your sins, there will still be some people who cannot forgive you. If God has forgiven you, you need to move on and simply accept that these people have a right to their opinion. Do your best to make the situation "right" if you can, and then go on with your life committed to being a light in a dark world.

Do not let their unforgiveness hinder *you* from being God's instrument and using you to fulfill His plan.

You may never be able to change other people's feelings or their opinion of you, but try not to hold it against them. Sadly, many Christians find that people can be downright unforgiving and unforgetting—refusing to move forward and continually raising past issues or throwing your past sins up in your face. Though you may have completely turned your life around, there will always be some people who will doubt your sincerity or simply refuse to believe you could change.

When you encounter people like that, try to remember the story of Mary Magdalene in the Bible. Mary had a sordid past, yet aside from His mother, she was probably the woman who was closest to Jesus on this earth. There is no doubt Jesus forgave Mary Magdalene her sins, and He forgives yours, too.

Back in Jesus' day, people didn't understand the power of His love to turn Mary Magdalene's life around, and they may not understand the effect of His love and forgiveness on *your* life today either. There just isn't much of anything we can do about that. Accept it, pray that God might change their hearts, and move on.

Pass It On

That's when it is more important than ever to remember that God has called us to love and forgive others (even our "enemies" or people who seem to hate us). In the face of someone else judging us and refusing to give us the benefit of the doubt, we are called to forgive *them* their hard feelings towards us. Even when they do not acknowledge or accept our repentance.

Likewise, when someone else hurts you or does something to anger you, you need to remember how God forgave you and commit your life to forgiving those who have hurt you. Even though others may withhold their forgiveness or hold a grudge against you, you must not withhold forgiveness from them.

Perhaps the chain of forgiveness begins with you. Maybe your taking the first step will be the catalyst that helps that person discover God and forgiveness in their own life. But there are no guarantees. They may just as easily rebuff you. It doesn't matter. You are still called to forgive them in your heart and move forward with your life—in the direction God guides you to go.

- ✞ Do you truly and fully accept that Jesus died on the cross to save you from your sins?
- ✞ Do you fully accept His gift of forgiveness?
- ✞ Do you forgive yourself for your sins?
- ✞ Can you forgive others who hurt you as Jesus forgave you?
- ✞ Who do you need to forgive today?
- ✞ Who do you need to ask forgiveness from?

Pray With Me...

Dear Lord,
It is unimaginable to me that your Son—pure and innocent—had to die a horrible death on the cross for *me*, to pay for *my* sins. I cannot even begin to imagine the pain of it. Nothing I can ever do will even begin to repay you for the gift of my salvation.

Thank you, Lord, for your wonderful gift of eternal life through Jesus. Guide me to share that gift with others by forgiving them the hurt they've caused me and sharing the story of your Son with people who do not yet know you or believe so that they, too, can enjoy the gift of everlasting life.

Amen

Chapter 9:
God Answers Every Prayer

Does He Hear You?

For some people, prayer can be a difficult concept to understand. Speaking or communicating with a being or power—our God—that they cannot hear, see, or touch is difficult to comprehend. Those of us who believe do so by faith—and sometimes we even have to pray for a stronger faith to go on believing. It is so easy to doubt—to question whether our prayers have been heard or answered.

Some people were never introduced to God, never taught to believe, and never given the opportunity to learn about His love. To hear about a God they never knew and to believe in Him is hard to imagine and accept. As adults it may be easier to doubt than to trust.

Many who are introduced to God will reject Him and His promises in favor of a secular lifestyle and modern beliefs. Yet, Christianity continues to exist.

And prayer continues to be the most powerful source we can draw on if only we knew how to use it.

God Answers *All* Prayers

God hears and responds to every prayer we send heavenward, no matter how great or how small. He listens to our pleas and praise, and He knows our needs and our prayers even before we say them.

Sometimes people will say their prayers go unanswered, but there really is no such thing. God always, always answers our prayers. Sometimes He grants our requests quickly and easily. At other times, the answer is not what we want to hear or is not so easy to decipher. We may not be entirely clear about what He is trying to tell us. But in every case, there is absolutely no denying our prayers are heard and answered.

Will Prayer Give Me Everything I Want?

Does praying mean you will always get everything you want? Does it mean you will have whatever material things you desire and ask for, that whatever whim crosses your mind, you have only to ask for it and God will grant it? Will He send you $1 million? Will you get the big, fancy house you've always wanted? Will you wear designer clothes and drive an expensive car?

Well, there may be circumstances that will lead to your winning $1 million, owning an impressive home, and living an impressive lifestyle, but prayer isn't a lottery ticket or a handful of magic beans. It isn't a quick fix for getting everything you've ever desired in terms of worldly possessions and wealth.

No. God is also not the Bank of America. Neither is He a loan officer or the tooth fairy leaving money under your pillow or Santa Claus with an endless supply of presents piled under your tree.

Prayers for money and possessions may not be readily answered in the form of cash to spare and a limitless credit card.

You are unlikely to win the lottery just because you really *want* to and you pray that you will.

God may not always give you what you *want,* but He *will* always give you what you *need.*

Think about all the stories in the Bible. Remember when the disciples were fishing all day without catching anything and Jesus told them where to cast their nets so they would find fish? Remember when he fed 4,000 people with just seven loaves and a few small fish? Remember the manna in the desert? The Bible is filled with proof that God always provides for His people, His children.

God is our Father, and a very caring Father He is. He will not spoil us—His children—and encourage us to run wild and out of control, becoming greedy and self-indulgent. In fact, when we pray for something we ought not to have, He may very well tell us flat out "no." Wouldn't we do the same for our children? If we love them, we would. A wise and loving parent knows that giving our children every little thing they desire is not good for them. And so the Father knows that giving us all lots of money and material possessions is not always good for us, either.

Our God loves *us* even more than we love our children. He loves us more than we can ever comprehend. In His wisdom, He answers our prayers according to what is best for us.

A Loving Father is Wise

We've all prayed for blessings we haven't received. Sometimes it is easy to get discouraged and wonder if God even hears our prayers and if He is really listening.

God does hear and respond to every one of our prayers and requests. But like the loving father that He is, sometimes He simply cannot say "yes" when we ask for what is not in our best interests or in His plan for us.

Our God is a wise and wonderful God who knows what is best for all His children. As mothers, most of us can relate to that. We do not give our children everything we ask for *because* we love them. This is one of the ways we actually show our love and commitment to our children.

So, too, does God. He knows what we need far better than we do, and He answers our prayers according to His great love for us and His plan for our lives.

When God Says No

God is the perfect parent. As the wise and perfect parent He is, He recognizes that some of the things we pray for are not good for us—they are not in our own best interest or they are not in His plan for our life.

God's ways are not our ways. He holds the great plan for all of us—the road map for life—a plan we cannot see. We see only a small part of the big picture. Our immediate needs, wants, and desires are in the forefront of our minds.

We cannot see beyond the short road that lies ahead of us, and we pray to God accordingly. But He knows what we will encounter on our journey through life—miles beyond what we can see now. He has a greater plan that we cannot fully comprehend. We must trust in His wisdom.

Often, we pray for things that are not in our own best interests—sometimes knowingly, like spoiled children, but often without any awareness at all. God sees our future clearly and has a plan for each of us.

He may tell us "no" to a prayer request because He has something different and much better in mind for us in the future.

He often says "no" to spare us incredible heartache and disappointment, all of which we know nothing about at the time. (Think about that guy you really wanted to marry in high school—look at him now. What if God had said yes to that prayer? Need I say more?)

Sometimes, He says "no" to our prayers because there is a lesson we need to learn.

Difficulties often present themselves as opportunities to grow and change, to become a better person and a better Christian. God knows there are lessons we need to learn, trials we must endure to grow. He understands our pain and our desire to have an "easy" life, but without these difficulties or challenges to help us grow, we would not learn important lessons—we would not mature in our faith.

Though it can be temporarily painful, God does have a plan for us. He does know what He's doing. When he tells us "no," it is for our greater good—to fulfill His will for our lives.

We don't like to hear "no." So we persist, pestering Him again and again with the same prayers, imploring Him to give us our way. But thankfully, like the wise and loving Father He is, God doesn't give in to our bullying. He holds firm to the path He has created for our lives.

Some things we pray for fervently are never meant to be—babies, relationships, jobs or opportunities we want—and we may never understand why while we are on this side of heaven. Other things we will come to understand with the passing of time. In the end, we are grateful for His firm hand when we realize what might have been.

Then, too, how can we appreciate the radiant glow of sunlight on our face if we have never known darkness? How can we fully know joy if we never felt sadness or knew pain or disappointment?

"Not Yet."

Sometimes God postpones the fulfillment of our prayers until the time is right. He gives us what we need in His time, not ours. While it may seem as if your prayers are not being answered, you can rest assured they are. God's immediate answer may simply be "not yet." Often God is whispering, "Just wait and see what I have planned for you."

Watch and wait. In time, you may receive what you have prayed faithfully for. Often, you will receive even more than you dared hope. God may have something even better and more wonderful in store for us than we could ever have imagined for ourselves. Have patience and trust in Him. He always knows what is best for us.

The answers to our prayers do not always come in the way that we expect them. God's way is not necessarily our way. We must learn to look beyond our specific requests to try to discern God's will for our lives and His long-term plan for us.

God First

During times when we don't sense God's immediate and affirmative response to our prayers, we must continue to pray and to draw our strength from Him. We need to remember that He knows the plan for all eternity, a plan we cannot even begin to comprehend.

It is during difficult times of waiting when I finally get to the point where I can give it all to God—as I should have in the first place—without trying to take it back. God *wants* to help us. He *wants* to help *you*. But He can't work on the situation if you won't give it to Him.

So give Him your worries, your troubles, and your pain. Give Him your problems and concerns and everything that is weighing you down. He can handle it.

Talk with Him and share your frustrations. It is OK to be confused, upset, hurt, and even angry with God. Go to Him. Speak to Him. Tell Him how you feel. Cry out to Him. Just don't turn away from Him. Turn *to* Him and ask Him for the strength you need to get through whatever you are dealing with.

Even Jesus, God's own son, on the cross of Calvary cried out to God in anguish—*"...My God, my God, why have you forsaken me?"*
Mathew 27:46

We are only human. We do not have divine understanding. In that moment, the humanity of Jesus was evident. In His suffering, He endured all that we have endured and have yet to endure. He suffered on our behalf. Jesus understands what we are going through. It's OK to get frustrated, come to Him with our problems, and "drop it all on God's doorstep."

Our weakness is made perfect in God.

Just don't turn away from Him.

God's Will be Done

When we pray, we will not always get the answers we want. Sometimes God says "yes" to our prayers. At other times, His answer is "no." And still others, He replies "not yet—wait and see what I have in store for you."

No matter how badly we want something, knowing that God has a greater plan and also knowing that He is omnipotent and eternal, we must always defer our prayers to God's will.

In other words, pray for what you want, but always end your prayer—"not mine but *Your* will be done." In order for God to do His work in our lives, we need to give Him the opportunity to work. We cannot dictate to Him.

Ask God to show you His will. Ask Him to give you strength. Ask Him to point you in the right direction, to help you focus on what He wants you to do, to bring some good out of every situation.

And we know that in all things God works for the good of those who love him, who have been called according to his purpose. Romans 8:28

He who did not spare his own Son, but gave him up for us all—how will He not also, along with him, graciously give us all things. Romans 8:32

Ask Him to *guide* you to do His will. Then leave it in His hands and accept His decision lovingly and graciously.

Of course, this is much easier said than done. As human beings, we are spoiled. We automatically assume that because we ask for something, we should receive it, and God should cooperate with *our* plans or whims.

I know that I am not a very patient person. I want what I want when I want it, much like a spoiled child. I have even been known to pray to God for patience, saying, "Please, Lord, give me patience, and I want it right NOW!" Shame on me. But He forgives me. Our loving, all-knowing Father forgives, forgets, and goes right on about His business, doing what is best for us despite all our whining and complaining about what we want.

No, God's ways are not our ways. God has a bigger, better plan. He knows things we do not know. He knows what is in our best interests more than we do. We can only see the small view.

When you pray, it is OK to ask God for what you want, but also understand that God's plan may not be your plan. His plan is based on the "big picture" and you may not be able to see that right now. He has the road map for your life, and He can see what's around the bend, even though you can't. So always express your willingness to accept God's will for your life and in response to your specific prayers, even if it is not what you asked for. Be willing to take what God gives you. It could be better than what you asked for in the first place.

When Bad Things Happen

Of course, everything that happens in our lives will not be good and joyous. During our time on earth, we will experience pain and suffering, grief and loss, sadness and loneliness.

One thing after another seems to go wrong, and even though we pray faithfully, we cannot see His hand at work in our lives, and we wonder if He hears us at all. Rest assured. He hears our cries. He hears all of our prayers.

Perhaps at times like these, God is testing us. Sure, it is easy to be faithful, good, and observant when everything is going fine. But what about when things are not so fine? Will we be faithful to Him then or will we turn on Him or turn *from* Him?

Do not despair. He is still there, still loving us, caring for us, watching over us, and He still has His arms around us even if we can't see them. If we stumble and fall, He will pick us up again, dust us off, and set us back on the right path.

With faith, patience, and the passing of time, He will get us through the tough times until we can once again rejoice and celebrate the blessings He gives us.

Besides being our loving Father, God is also our very best friend. He will only do what is in our best interest. Sure, there are some lessons we will have to learn along the way. And what is so surprising about that? Don't all good fathers have to teach their children? And so He teaches us. But does that mean He loves us any less? No.

So do not give up. Keep the faith. Trust in the Lord.

One of my favorite Bible verses to repeat when things seem to be going badly or when I am fearful and don't know what to do is in Proverbs.

Trust in the Lord with all your heart and lean not on your own understanding; in all your ways acknowledge him, and he will make your paths straight. Proverbs 3:15

I don't always know what's going to happen next, how things will turn out, or why things happen as they do. But God does. And that should be enough.

Let Go, Let God

True peace comes to us when we learn to let go and let God—when we place everything in God's capable hands and trust that it will all turn out OK because He is in charge. For many of us, this can be very difficult. As women, we are often charged with orchestrating family events, running a household, scheduling appointments, and keeping track of dozens of different things at once. Letting go is particularly hard for women who want to feel like they are in control of their lives and those who like to live by a schedule and don't particularly relish unexpected surprises.

Someone once suggested we need to work like everything is in our hands and pray like everything is in God's hands.

Ask God to help you do your very best in everything you do, but remember that the *results* are in God's hands. And what better hands could they be in?

- ✞ Do you pray for what you desire but end your prayers asking God to answer your prayers according to His will and plan for your life?
- ✞ Are you open to surprises in your life from God? Or are you so set in your ways that you cannot see some of God's hidden blessings in your life?
- ✞ Do you trust that God will do what is best for you?
- ✞ Can you thank God for answering your prayers even when His answer is "no" or "not yet?"
- ✞ Do you keep the faith even when it is not immediately evident whether your request will be granted?
- ✞ When you are struggling with difficulties in your life, do you turn to God for comfort and support?
- ✞ Is Jesus your very best friend or some distant unknown entity? How would you talk to your best friend? What

would you talk about? Can you open your heart to Jesus like you would to your best earthly friend?

Pray With Me...

Dear Lord,
Sometimes I grow impatient with you when I pray and do not receive an immediate response or when your reply is not what I wanted to hear. I don't like to hear "no" or "just wait a while" when I come to you. I much prefer it when you give me what I want when I want it.

And yet, I do realize that you are my loving Father in heaven and you have a greater plan—a plan that I cannot see and do not understand—and that you always do what is best for me, even if it is difficult for me at the time.

Help me to accept your will for my life lovingly and graciously and to follow you joyfully and without question. Put my doubts to rest and grant me the peace that only you can give.
Amen

Chapter 10: Listening For His Voice

Can You Hear Him?

How do you know when God is answering your prayers? How do you know it is His voice you hear, not just your own thoughts in your head, not just what you want to hear? How can you recognize His will?

Though He knows you intimately, you may not be familiar with Him. Or perhaps you are too troubled to feel His presence.

If this I the case, ask Him to calm you and let you feel His gentle love. Ask Him to help you become more open to receiving Him. And invite Him into your life, your heart, your soul.

You may not be able to feel His abiding presence immediately if this is unfamiliar territory to you. Don't worry. Like I said, He is there. Just continue on.

Prayer is a means of communicating with God and God with you. It is a two-way process. You speak to God and He listens. God also speaks to you, and you must hear in your heart and soul what He is saying to you. Since God gives us free will, He's probably waiting for you to make the first move in this conversation. Or perhaps you hear Him softly whisper to your soul in the words of Matthew 11:28, *"Come to me, all you who are weary and burdened, and I will give you rest."*

If the longing to communicate with God moves you, you can be assured that this is God at work in your soul.

Talk with God just as you would talk with a trusted and beloved friend and confidante. Withhold nothing. He knows it all anyway. You do not need to talk in any particularly eloquent way, in poetry or verse. God understands your language. Tell Him what's on your mind. Pour your heart out to Him and know that He understands. Share your troubles and concerns and ask for His guidance in your life. Ask Him to show you the way.

Listen Carefully

Ask Him. Then listen. Be present in the moment. Focus on what is happening right now. What is your intuition telling you? What is God saying to you right now? Your intuition is God's voice speaking from your soul. Learn to listen to that voice.

If you don't hear that voice immediately, or if you are not sure if it is God, open your Bible and begin reading. Sometimes if you pray before you open your Bible, God will direct you to a passage that will clearly show you His will.

If you are still in doubt, consider what Jesus would do in your circumstances. Often the answer to your prayers will become clear.

Give It All To God

The most effective prayers are those that we give over entirely to God. This sounds easy but often it is not. Jesus tells us to bring our problems to Him. But often, even when we do come to Him, we try to meddle in things too much ourselves. Like the story of the child who took a broken toy to God to be fixed and then kept taking it back, God says of our problems, "Now how could I fix it when you never would let go of it?" Give it to God in its entirety. Trust and let go.

"...Ask and it will be given to you; seek and you will find; knock and the door will be opened to you." Luke 11:9

If you take it back, you make it impossible for Him to work on the problem.

The Lord Works in Mysterious Ways

By the same token, don't be close-minded to the way God chooses to answer your prayers. Sometimes He answers and we do not recognize Him in our lives.

The Lord works in mysterious ways—often through His people on earth—to grant our requests, answer our prayers, and provide for our needs.

Modern medicine is probably the single greatest example of God at work through His people. The very best physicians we have today are quick to point out that although they administer the medicine or the treatment, it is always God who does the healing. God gives doctors the knowledge they need to facilitate the healing process. But He alone performs miracles. He alone heals.

Still, God often calls the physician to play a critical role. When a woman is diagnosed with breast cancer, she prays to God to save her from the disease. While there have been documented cases of inexplicable remissions and healings, chances are that God will use a doctor to facilitate her healing if that is His plan for her life.

God gives her physician the knowledge and wisdom he needs to make a diagnosis and a recommendation for treatment. Should the woman refuse the treatment, it is possible that she is refusing God's answer to her prayers for a longer life.

Always stay open to God's plan for your life. In His wisdom, he often answers our prayers in ways we do not anticipate.

Can You See God At Work?

There is a story of a man who lived in an area that was overcome by a flood. As the waters in the area began to rise, the man prayed to God to save him from the flood. Neighbors began to evacuate the area and as they left, they asked him to leave with them. But the man replied, "No, I know that God will save me."

As the waters continued to rise, the man climbed to the second story of his house and began praying again. Just then, some men came by in a boat and called to him. "No," he said, waving them on. "I don't need any help. God will save me."

Finally, to escape the rising, swirling waters, the man climbed to the roof of his house and prayed again to God to save him. A helicopter flew overhead and lowered a rope calling down to him, "Grab hold of the rope and we will rescue you." "No," replied the man. "God will save me."

Eventually the waters swirled even higher, and the man drowned. When he got to heaven, the man stood before God perplexed. "During the flood," he asked God, "I had such great faith in you. I was sure you would save me. Why didn't you?"

And God replied, "Three times I sent people to save you and remove you from danger, and you would not listen to them. What more could I do?"

Yes, just like this man, sometimes God sends us the answer to our prayers and we do not see it. The answers to our prayers do not always come in the way that we expect them. God's way is not necessarily our way. We must not be so stubborn and narrow minded that we cannot see God's blessings when He gives them to us.

Listen. Trust. Believe.

It seemed much simpler in the days of the Old Testament. God performed miracles in the Bible. He spoke to His people loud and clear.

I do not "hear" an audible voice, yet I hear Him "speak" to my soul. We communicate. Why is it so hard to believe God could communicate with Noah, Jonah, Moses, and others thousands of years ago but He cannot communicate with us today?

- ✞ Do you listen to hear what God is telling you?
- ✞ Can you decipher between God's will for your life and your own selfish desires?
- ✞ Are you looking for the miracles in your life?
- ✞ Do you recognize God's answers to your prayers even when they come to you through other people or in ways you don't expect?

Pray With Me...

Dear Lord,
I long to hear your voice, to know clearly what you want me to do and how you want me to live my life. Sometimes I am not certain if I am doing what you want me to do. I don't always know if I am reading your signs correctly or if I am interpreting things the way *I* want them to be.

Help me to discern your voice from my own desires, to interpret your answers to my prayers clearly, and to do your will with a joyful heart.
Amen

Chapter 11: Walking By Faith

Prayer Restores Us

In our hectic everyday lives, we can easily become preoccupied with all the trivial things we have to do and overwhelmed by the burdens of daily living. Prayer provides us with a blessed intervention. It cushions and protects us from the rest of the world with a layer of peace that surrounds us—God's peace.

We share in His wisdom and begin to understand that all the things of this world and the life we have today, no matter how good, bad, or in between, will one day be replaced by a life that is so much more meaningful and blessed than anything we could ever imagine. He is guiding us toward eternal life with Him.

But even along the way, here on earth He guides our steps and helps us to prioritize our daily responsibilities and activities—if we ask Him for that guidance. And He is, oh, so happy to give it to us! All we have to do is ask.

Every Little Thing

We can ask for God's blessing and guidance in each and every area of our lives, no matter how large or how small.

Some of us think that God is an Almighty power we can call upon in times of great stress or loss. Somehow we grew up thinking that God wasn't to be "bothered" with the small stuff. He had *big* problems to take care of.

But the belief that God is available only to call on in times of trouble or when you need to bring in the "big guns" is totally unfounded. God wants to be involved in every single area of your life. He wants to bless you and guide you beyond your wildest dreams.

But because He gave us free will, He will not push Himself into your life unwelcomed. You must invite Him in. It is so simple to do. All you have to do is ask. And He will be there with you, every step of the way, right by your side, day and night— protecting you, guiding you, intervening on your behalf, and blessing you. He gives us the most precious gift of all—unconditional and complete love and acceptance.

You are precious in His sight. He has so many gifts to give you. But you must be willing to open your heart and soul and receive them. You have to want Him in your life and ask Him into your life.

"Here I am! I stand at the door and knock. If anyone hears my voice and opens the door, I will come in and eat with him, and he with me." Revelations 3:20

Just a Little Faith

God is a good and loving God. All He requires is a little faith. Do not be worried that your faith is not strong enough. Remember that Jesus Himself tells us that if we have even the faith of a mustard seed, we can believe and our prayers will be answered.

"I tell you the truth, if you have faith as small as a mustard seed, you can say to this mountain, 'Move from here to there' and it will move. Nothing will be impossible for you." Matthew 17:20)

And as your prayer life—and your relationship with God—grows and develops, your faith will increase without effort. You can also pray for more faith and trust in Him.

...the Spirit helps us in our weakness. We do not know what we ought to pray for, but the Spirit himself intercedes for us with groans that words cannot express. And he who searches our hearts knows the mind of the Spirit, because the Spirit intercedes for the saints in accordance with God's will. Romans 8:26-27

My faith has evolved over time. It has grown stronger because of the disappointments and struggles I have dealt with along the way. There are many things I have done that I am not proud of, but I think God used those things as opportunities for me to grow. If I hadn't gone through them, I don't think I could be as spiritually strong as I am today. If life had been easy and pain-free, I would not have gained the wisdom He's given me.

Through each of my trials, God showed me the way—His way. If I had not been a horrible sinner, I would not have fallen. If I had not fallen, I would have thought I could walk life's path on my own. I would not have needed Jesus as desperately as I did.

But because I was without any doubt a sinner, I could not do it alone. I had to have help. So God sent me His Son to show me the way. The only way.

Jesus answered, "I am the way and the truth and the life. No one comes to the Father except through me." John 14:6

One Day At a Time

After you begin praying regularly and develop a relationship with God, you will reach a place of peace and contentment. You will go for a while—sometimes a long while—and think you've mastered the process. But then, the inevitable happens. You will trip and fall.

Even ministers and people of strong spiritual fiber stumble along the way. You will become discouraged, disheartened, and doubtful. Perhaps you will become complacent or a bit numb to the workings of the Holy Spirit in your life.

Like a new penny that has been riding around in your pocket for a while, the shine will begin to wear off, and you may not feel the same sense of excitement about your faith as you used to. That special glow you emitted when you first found God may seem to have dimmed.

This is a sign that you need to recharge your spiritual batteries, refresh your spirit, and replenish your soul.

We are only human, and as such, our faith can and will ebb and flow. We are not perfect like God. Only He is perfect and consistent, without ups and downs, highs and lows. And in our humanity, our prayer life and our spiritual life are also subject to those ups and downs.

There will be times when we feel strong in our faith and other times when we feel weak and unsure. This is just one of the reasons it is important to spend time with other Christians— to support one another during our low points and to help to strengthen one another.

Begin Again

During these times, we simply must start over and begin the process again, turning to God to give us the strength and faith we lack—to show us the way once more. In our lives, we will go through this process many times. Along the way, God places little reminders to help us—perhaps the words in a song that strike a chord in our soul, reminding us of our emptiness and the God that can fill us and make us whole—the words that bring us back to Him.

Perhaps it is a tragedy or sorrow or hearing the story of someone less fortunate than us that reminds us how blessed we truly are.

It may be an accident or illness that makes us realize how far we have drifted from God's plan for our lives.

We may simply feel depressed, lost, and alone until a scripture verse or a word from a friend reminds us that we are never alone. We can invite Jesus into our heart and find complete fulfillment. So we ask Him in again.

Not all Sunshine and Roses

Just because we pray, God doesn't promise that all obstacles will be lifted from our paths, that everything will be sunshine and roses, and that we will be free from all problems.

On the contrary, sometimes living our faith in God and sharing our love for Jesus can make Christians targets for persecution. In many parts of the world, this is still so. Even in the United States, when freedom of speech supposedly grants rights to everyone to speak their minds, Christians are often squelched and discriminated against in subtle ways.

For instance, in trying to promote *Obadiah Magazine*, a Christian magazine my friend, LaDonna Meredith, and I own in partnership, we were encouraged to downplay the Christianity aspect and focus more on the fact that we met and started our business on the Internet to get secular publicity opportunities. Sometimes the only way to reach out to people in God's love is by downplaying our wonderful message so that people will listen without shutting us out, and then slowly introduce them to the Savior when they are ready—when they come to trust us and are more receptive.

The secular world may not be ready for the Savior, and getting in their face won't make them any more accepting. We need to be quiet, gentle, and subtle when we make our case for Christ—just as Jesus was.

Prayer is not black magic. It is not a potion or a cure-all solution to be applied like a bandage to our lives.

Prayer will not eliminate the bills we need to pay, health problems, marital discord, or bad things happening to good people—for all these things are ways of the world and are a part of being human. Right now we are in the world and we are human, so we must abide by the natural laws of this world.

But God creates His own laws, and He does not need to abide by the laws of our earthly existence or the man-made laws that govern us here. Through prayer, we can tap into *His* power.

On Difficult Days...

God tells us that His strength is made perfect in our weakness. Even if all of our troubles don't disappear, God will give us the strength to deal with and overcome them. He can do it. And He will, too.

Remember, this is the God who has overcome the world. He can help us get through our difficult days and tough spots, too.

When we turn to God for help and guidance in our lives, we are tapping into the greatest power source in all the universe, in all of time. His strength is enormous. We cannot even begin to imagine it.

Does God Ever Give Us More Than We Can Handle?

I've often heard it said that God never gives us more than we can handle. Sometimes I've even said it myself.

But the plain and simple truth is, He does. Oftentimes, many of the challenges, sorrows, and catastrophes we encounter are way too much for us to handle. These things threaten to crush us. *But* God never gives us more than we *and He* can handle *together.*

When our strength cannot take us further, God's strength is always sufficient for us. He has more than enough.

Praying will not take all your troubles away. But it will bring God closer to you. By inviting God to be an active, personal part of your life, your troubles will no longer have a hold on you. They will lose their power in deference to God's almighty power.

Your troubles will become more like nuisances than critical problems when you know God is in control.

And we know that in all things God works for the good of those who love him, who have been called according to his purpose. Romans 8:28

Like the eagle that flies above the storm, we can rise above our troubles in this life when we call on God to help us. We don't have to let our storms beat us down. If we ask Him, God can lift us above our worries and help us ride the winds of sickness and death, tragedy and sorrow, failure and disappointment. We place our hope and faith in God's strength to bring us through.

...but those who hope in the Lord will renew their strength. They will soar on wings like eagles; they will run and not grow weary, they will walk and not be faint. Isaiah 40:29

God can take bad situations and turn them around. He can turn sorrow into joy, tears into laughter, and death into life. Such is the kingdom of God. Because *"...all things are possible with God."* Mark 10:27

Let Him Shower You With Blessings

God *wants* to bless you and shower you with His love. He wants you to honor and love Him in return. He wants to be first in your life.

Take some special time each and every day to spend with your Lord. Perhaps it is at the end of the day, soaking in a hot bathtub, when you finally have the chance to clear your mind, share your thoughts with Him, and to thank Him for the blessings of the day and for watching over you and your loved ones. It is then that you pray again for His blessed intervention for those who call upon and need Him, and in these quiet minutes you listen closely for His direction in your life.

When you pray, no matter where that may be—in a quiet bathroom, in a busy subway, or in a crowded restaurant—focus as closely and sincerely as you can on God, and try to block other thoughts from your mind. Share with Him, talk with Him, focus on Him, thank Him, praise Him, worship Him, ask Him, love Him. Put Him first.

We need to put God first in all areas of our life. We need to consider each thing we do, think, or say from God's perspective. What would *He* want you to do. When you are faced with decisions, *ask* Him for guidance and direction in making the right choices.

Give God the opportunity, and He will bless you so abundantly that you won't know what hit you! Then rest easy in knowing that faithfulness and prayer evolve with time and practice and we all make mistakes along the way. The wonderful thing is—God already knows this and He won't hold it against us.

A Work in Progress

I like to say that I am a work in progress— constantly evolving, changing, and growing. That's why I'm still here.

I tell myself that all things will come to those who wait. But in reality I am not very patient about my progress or about waiting.

We need to constantly remind ourselves that God's time is not our time. All things will come to pass in God's time, not ours.

- ✝ Do you grow impatient with your spiritual progress?
- ✝ Did you think praying would "fix" all of your problems and that believing would make your life "easy?"
- ✝ Is God really first in your life? What do your actions say is first in your life? (Remember, actions speak much louder than words.)
- ✝ Do you have a supportive network of Christians who can help you when you are struggling in your faith?
- ✝ Are you making a little more progress in your faith each day?

Pray With Me...

Dear Lord,
When I first started praying to you, the excitement overwhelmed me. I prayed. I read your Word. I sought your wisdom in every area of my life.

I thought that with you here beside me, life would get a lot better. It was hard for me to accept the fact that sometimes my *circumstances* wouldn't actually change. Sometimes they even got *worse!* But your love saw me through it all. I couldn't have done it without you. Your love and peace gave me the strength I needed to deal with the circumstances.

Then the difficulties passed and things went along smoothly for a while. I forgot to pray quite as often—after all, things were going fine and I wasn't in nearly as much distress. Gradually my prayer time was replaced with other "things" that needed to be done.

Now I realize that my priorities need to be "God first" so that I can continue to grow in your love. Now I know that my prayer time with you is precious. It is the cool drink of water on a long hot day. It is what sustains me despite all the difficulties of this world.

Thank you for bringing me back to you, Jesus. Thank you for your gift of salvation. Thank you for your peace. Help me to be ever mindful of how much I love and need your daily companionship and guidance. Help me to put you first in my life, always and forever.

Amen

Chapter 12:
Do Not Worry

Feeling Overwhelmed?

The bills are piling up and the kids need new shoes. The car is making a funny noise, but you're too nervous about how you'd pay for service to make an appointment at the shop—you just try to ignore it hoping it will go away. Your daughter is late getting home and hasn't called, and you're worried sick.

Hundreds of little things like this can cause us stress—day in and day out. We worry about family, friends, finances, our health and our jobs, and dozens of other things too numerous to mention. Most of our worry is totally wasted—because nine times out of ten, the things that we worry about never do happen.

It's almost funny in a way—how much time we spend fretting and fussing over something that never actually occurs. The only trauma is in our heads and our hearts.

But it's not really funny, because worry and stress cause an untold number of health problems for people every year—from migraines to upset stomachs and ulcers, heart disease to back and neck pain, and twitching nerves to breaking out in a rash. Health problems created by or exacerbated by stress affect millions of people.

Why do we worry so much? If we worry, will it change the way things actually happen? Or will it just rob us of a peaceful moment in the present? One way or the other, we will need to deal with things as they happen, right? So why do we let ourselves get worked up about things that *might*—but seldom actually ever do—happen?

God's Wisdom on Worry

God knows our lives here on earth are stressful, but He urges us to trust in Him. In fact, He even tells us straight out that we shouldn't worry. He is in control, and we really have nothing to worry about.

Thousands of years before the invention of cell phones, pagers, credit cards, and all the other devices that speed the pace of present-day life to a frenzy, God knew we needed to set our worries aside, and He told us to bring them to Him so that He could handle them for us. He assured us of His love and protection for us and even assured us that He would provide for our every need.

"Therefore I tell you, do not worry about your life, what you will eat or drink; or about your body, what you will wear. Is not life more important than food, and the body more important than clothes? Look at the birds of the air; they do not sow or reap or store away in barns, and yet your heavenly Father feeds them. Are you not much more valuable than they? Who of you by worrying can add a single hour to his life?" Matthew 6:25-27

"So do not worry, saying 'What shall we eat?' or 'What shall we drink?' or 'What shall we wear?'" Matthew 6:31

"But seek first his righteousness, and all these things will be given to you as well. Therefore do not worry about tomorrow, for tomorrow will worry about itself. Each day has enough trouble of its own." Matthew 6:33-34

"Are not two sparrows sold for a penny? Yet not one of them will fall to the ground apart from the will of your Father." Matthew 10:29

"So don't be afraid; you are worth more than many sparrows." Matthew 10:30

"And even the very hairs of your head are all numbered." Matthew 10:30

"Come to me, all you who are weary and burdened, and I will give you rest. Take my yoke upon you and learn from me, for I am gentle and humble in heart, and you will find rest for your souls." Matthew 11:28-29

"Trust in the Lord with all your heart and lean not on your own understanding; in all your ways acknowledge him, and he will make your paths straight." Proverbs 3:5-6

...If God is for us, who can be against us? Romans 8:31

Only One

Even at our very lowest and most distraught, when everything seems hopeless and we can't seem to find a way out, God is there for us.

There is only One who can pick you up and bring you peace. He is our all-knowing Father in heaven.

Things will happen on this earth, and we may not know why. Bad things happen to seemingly good people. Yet despite all these things and all that we do not know, if we have faith, God can help us cope with it. He can carry us through.

Do you remember the "Footprints" poem? I don't know who wrote it, but it tells the story of a man who had a dream that he was walking along a beach talking with the Lord. He and the Lord walked and talked, and at the same time they looked back over the scenes of the man's life on earth. As he watched the scenes of his life flash before him, he noticed two sets of footprints in the sand—one that belonged to him and the other belonging to Jesus as Jesus walked beside him throughout his life.

But the man noticed that at the lowest and most difficult times in his life, there was only one set of footprints. The man, like many of us human beings are inclined to do, became upset and asked the Lord why—at the lowest and most awful and difficult moments in his life—he had deserted him. "How could you?" we can almost hear him ask. "I trusted you, and you let me down. Where *were* you?"

If you've read the poem, you may remember how Jesus replied. "My precious, precious child…," he said. (And notice there was no anger or resentment in His voice for having been accused of abandoning the man during his time of need.) "I love you and I would never leave you. During your times of trial and suffering, when you see only one set of footprints, it was then that I carried you."

It is a beautiful illustration, and aptly so. For it is during the most difficult moments in our lives—when we feel all alone and scared—that God is very present in our lives, waiting to help us and comfort us. He never leaves us or forsakes us.

There is no need for us to worry. God is always by our side. We only need to call on Him and He is right there, an ever present help in times of trouble.

The righteous cry out, and the Lord hears them; he delivers them from all their troubles. Psalm 34:17

A righteous man may have many troubles, but the Lord delivers him from them all. Psalm 34:19

"…call upon me in the day of trouble; I will deliver you, and you will honor me." Psalm 50:15

"Do not let your hearts be troubled. Trust in God; trust also in me." John 14:1

"Peace I leave with you; my peace I give you. I do not give to you as the world gives. Do not let your hearts be troubled and do not be afraid." John 14:27

Practical Advice to Combat Worry and Fear

That's all very well and good, I can hear you saying to yourself, *but not worrying is a lot easier said than done.* You're right, of course. It is. I've had my share of sleepless nights and irrational fears, worries over money problems and how we were ever going to get out from under our bills, and even "justifiable" worries when someone was seriously ill or injured.

It's one thing to *say* you're not going to worry and quite another to actually stop yourself from worrying.

You may find it helpful to commit one or more Bible verses dealing with worry to your memory. When you are caught in the grip of fear or worry—wherever you are—repeat the scripture verse over and over like a mantra, breathing in and out, and physically calming yourself. You can intersperse this with making yourself focus rationally on the fact that in the past when you have worried, your fears seldom came to pass. It really was a waste of your time to have allowed that fear and worry to take over last time, and it probably is this time, too.

My favorite scripture when I am really, really panicking about something is Proverbs 3:5. You may want to try that one or find a scripture that really speaks to you personally and has a calming effect on you.

If you are able, take some time to read God's Word in the Bible to help abate your worry, as well. Listen to some Christian music that can sooth your nerves and remind you of God's greatness and goodness—it will help you "let go" of your worries and give them to Him a little easier.

If you can, talk with a trusted Christian friend or counselor. Someone looking at your situation from the outside usually has a more objective perspective and can help reassure you and calm you down. Sometimes they can even impart practical advice and wisdom about what you can do to solve whatever it is you're worried about. At the very least, they can pray with you for God's peace in your heart.

- ✞ Do you often feel anxious or distressed?
- ✞ Is your life full of fear and worry?
- ✞ How do you deal with stress in your life?
- ✞ Do you know any scriptures (committed to memory) about trusting in God and letting go of fear and worry?
- ✞ Who is a trusted Christian friend you can call on for a rational perspective and a prayer when you need comfort?
- ✞ Do you talk through your troubles with God?
- ✞ Do you trust God to take care of you and your loved ones?
- ✞ Do you trust Him to provide for you?

Pray With Me...

Dear Lord,
It is so hard not to worry. All around us things are going on and sometimes they seem to spin out of control. I don't know what to do or how to deal with them.

The realities are bad enough, but then my imagination runs wild and I can work myself up into a real frenzy. Before I know it, I'm in a full-blown panic. Help me to *stop* and turn to you.

Remind me that most of the things I worry about never come to fruition. Help me remember that we are all still in your loving care, and even if things seem out of control to me, they are never out of *your* control. Remind me that no matter what happens, you will always be with me to help me and guide me, and there is nothing that you and I together can't handle.
Amen

Chapter 13:
Praying For Purpose

Discovering Your Calling

Do you have a calling? Of course, you do. If you don't know what it is, perhaps you simply haven't discovered it yet. Each and every one of us was placed on this earth for a very real and valid reason. God knew exactly what He was doing when He made you.

Still, many of us go about our daily lives rushing and running around with no idea of what our purpose is. We may not believe God has anything special in mind for us at all. We probably think we are just "us"—and God couldn't possibly have a mission or purpose in mind for little old "us."

The truth is, God has used everyday people—and women just like us—to do His work for centuries. And He is using women like us to do His work today.

If you don't know what God is calling you to do, spend some time in prayer to find out. You can pray that God will reveal His special plan for your life to you. He will help you call to mind the special gifts and talents He gave you to help fulfill this calling.

Gifts Come in All Shapes and Sizes

When considering the gifts God reveals to you, don't overlook the little things. Too often you may pass over some of the gifts you've been given because they come in odd-sized packages or they don't seem very impressive when compared to someone else's gifts.

But never underestimate God. He gave *you* your special gifts for a reason. They need not be fancy or impressive to a worldly audience to be suited to God's work.

Mother Theresa devoted her life to helping the poor. While she became well known, on the surface she didn't possess very impressive "gifts." She dressed simply, spoke softly, and went about her business of caring for people and ministering to them. She lived in poverty and devoted her life to other people in impoverished areas. She used her gifts of compassion and hard work to help God's people.

Some women possess a gift of teaching. Whether they teach a classroom of students or share God's love with a single person, they can use that gift to His glory through their teaching and educating others.

Nurses and doctors are blessed with gifts of healing. Some women are gifted listeners who can sympathize with and help others who are hurting. Some of you will find gifts that directly help others or serve God. Others will be gifted with talents that support other people who do His work.

Each and every one of us possesses at least one special gift or talent God has given us to glorify Him in some way.

Ask God to show you one of your gifts today. When you pray, thank Him for your gifts and pray for guidance and direction in using your gifts the way He wants you to.

We have different gifts, according to the grace given us. If a man's gift is prophesying, let him use it in proportion to his faith. If it is serving, let him serve; if it is teaching, let him teach; if it is contributing to the needs of others, let him give generously; if it is leadership, let him govern diligently; if it is showing mercy, let him do it cheerfully. Romans 12:6-8

Of course, I quoted directly from scripture, but God certainly means for women to use their gifts this way, too!

Start Where Your Heart Is

Each and every one of us was individually created by God with a very special purpose. But maybe you haven't found your purpose yet. Do you know why God created you and placed you on this earth?

Sometimes we cause ourselves a lot more stress than we need to trying to determine what our life mission or purpose is. It really doesn't have to be that difficult.

When God created us, He designed us with a built in passion for that which would be our purpose. When do you feel most happy? Most alive? What are you doing when you feel pure, true joy?

Chances are that your God-given mission is directly related to that which gives you the most satisfaction.

Some women find their mission in teaching, healing, preaching, or counseling. It may be in working with individuals, children, singles, women, men, families, or the elderly. Perhaps it is found working with the physically or mentally challenged, the sick, prisoners, or students.

Ministry and your mission can be developed in countless occupations and hobbies. When you're doing something, and you are doing it for God, *that* is part of your mission. Sometimes people simply overlook areas that may be a part of their calling.

Perhaps *you* take some of your gifts for granted and overlook them when, in fact, God gave them to you to be a part of your calling. A mission need not be directly related to a church ministry to be a part of God's plan. It need not be a high profile or highly visible activity to be a calling.

God's people are everywhere—behind the scenes—doing His work.

Some women are called to raise a good Christian family and set the course for their children's upbringing and future direction. Certainly, Mary, the mother of Jesus, was so called.

For other women, comforting others who are going through difficulties or grieving, or just listening when they need to talk, may be their calling. Perhaps it is cheering up someone who is depressed or helping someone come to Christ by saying just the right thing at the critical time. We will never know this side of heaven just how many lives and souls we touch in countless little ways and how that can make a difference for someone else's eternity.

You may possess a practical, hands-on talent or skill—like making quilts and blankets for homeless shelters, preparing layettes for newborns, reading to a child, caring for the elderly or hospice patients, adopting a foster child, holding someone's hand as they go through chemo, or cooking a meal for a disabled neighbor. It may be stamping cards to be sent to shut-ins, collating church bulletins or newsletters, writing letters for patients, or weeding a flower garden when a friend is ill.

The activity is not nearly so important as the fact that you are doing it to honor and glorify God and fulfilling His two greatest commandments: to love Him above all else and to love your neighbor as yourself.

"'Love the Lord your God with all your heart and with all your soul and with all your mind and with all your strength.' ... 'Love your neighbor as yourself.' There is no commandment greater than these." Mark 12: 30-31

Do It For God

Your life mission may not be the kind of activity or event that will attract a lot of attention from other people. It may not be very visible at all. It could be something you do in private—praying for others, caring for an elderly relative, or just calling someone who is lonely. It doesn't have to be something public or something others know about. In fact, God often works through us in very subtle, discreet ways.

God ordained each of us with a special purpose, and if we fulfill that purpose, it doesn't matter what value other human beings place on the achievement. God's scale of measurement and significance is the one that matters—not ours. We do not have the capacity to look at things the same way God does. We cannot always comprehend His ways.

Your individual purpose or mission may be to touch or to impact *one* life in a small but significant way. It may not be your calling to save hundreds of lives or bring thousands to Christ. Yet the one life you impact is just as significant to God.

Follow Your Calling

Find your God-given passion and pursue it. Serve the Lord with enthusiasm and joy. God does not require you to be miserable and suffering to complete your calling. There is nothing wrong with finding pleasure in the pursuit of God's mission for your life.

Live your life with joy and purpose. Celebrate your success! Thank God for His blessings!

Discover a purpose worth living for. Then set your goals, make your decisions, live your life, and make your choices all based on that ultimate purpose.

God wants us to live our lives to the fullest.

"...I have come that they may have life, and have it to the full." John 10:10

To be truly alive, you must have a purpose. A life purpose gives your life meaning, motivates you, and is a source of satisfaction and joy.

...Forgetting what is behind and straining toward what is ahead, I press on toward the goal to win the prize for which God has called me heavenward in Christ Jesus. Philippians 3:13-14

Every individual is unique. Every life and purpose is unique. There may be similarities between women, but the details are different. God created you for a special, individual purpose.

When you live your life according to your calling, you are fully and truly alive. Positive self-esteem stems from living a life of purpose.

Your Gifts Are Special

God makes each of us just a little bit differently. We are all individuals with specific likes and dislikes, talents, skills, and attributes. No two of us are exactly alike. In the same way, we all have different aptitudes, preferences, and desires.

God made you just the way you are in order to use you as He has planned.

What makes you feel happy, whole, alive, and fulfilled? What is your passion? Can this passion directly or indirectly be used for some good, God-serving purpose?

Could this be your personal calling? Your life's mission? Yes!

Service to God is any way we use our blessings from Him to help or minister to others. When you are serving God in the way He intended, you will experience peace, satisfaction, fulfillment, and joy. It may be challenging. It may be simple or profound. It may be enlightening or strictly functional. But in some way it will touch your heart and soul.

Often you will lose all track of time when you are doing God's work. Your motivation and inspiration levels will be high. You will know that your doing this not only brings you closer to

God because you are serving Him, but it also brings Him great joy.

Follow your heart to do God's calling. *Don't compare your gifts to other women's gifts. Don't think your gifts and your calling should be the same as theirs. Don't let anyone convince you that your gift is any less important than someone else's.*

There is no comparing God-given gifts. He needs us all. No one gift is any more or less important than another. We have all been called, and we all need each other, and God needs each of us to serve His purpose.

There are different kinds of gifts, but the same Spirit. There are different kinds of service, but the same Lord. There are different kinds of working, but the same God works all of them in all men.

Now to each one the manifestation of the Spirit is given for the common good. To one there is given through the Spirit the message of wisdom, to another the message of knowledge by means of the same Spirit, to another faith by the same Spirit, to another gifts of healing by that one Spirit, to another miraculous powers, to another prophecy, to another distinguishing between spirits, to another speaking in different kinds of tongues, and to still another the interpretation of tongues. All these are the work of one and the same Spirit, and he gives them to each one, just as he determines. 1 Corinthians 12:7-11

God needs each and every one of us, doing what we are called to do. Even the simple, little things that don't seem very grand on the surface are valuable in His sight.

"For I was hungry and you gave me something to eat, I was thirsty and you gave me something to drink, I was a stranger and you invited me in, I needed clothes and you clothed me, I was sick and you looked after me, I was in prison and you came to visit me...I tell you the truth, whatever you did for one of the least of these brothers of mine, you did for me." Matthew 25:35-36, 40

He Will Help You

Most of us never achieve anywhere near our full God-given potential because we don't ask Him to show us what that is and to help us.

Sometimes the task God calls us to do can seem too big for us to accomplish. Often after we are inspired with an idea, we still struggle with how to implement it and whether we are the right woman for the job.

Always remember that if God has truly called you to this purpose, He will make a way. He will help you blaze a trail to accomplish His work if that is what it takes.

...he who began a good work in you will carry it on to completion until the day of Christ Jesus. Philippians 1:6

...for it is God who works in you to will and to act according to his good purpose. Philippians 2:13

- ✞ Do you feel God guiding you toward a particular calling?
- ✞ Are you using your talents and skills in ways that glorify God and serve Him?
- ✞ Have you been putting off doing something you feel called to do out of feelings of insecurity?
- ✞ What kinds of things do you enjoy doing? Think of something that—when you're doing it—makes you absolutely lose track of time.
- ✞ Is there something you could/should be doing for others in Jesus' name that you have been avoiding?

Pray With Me...

Dear Lord,
You have given me so many gifts. Help me to remember that my talents and skills are not of my own making, but they are blessings you gave me and gifts I should use to honor and glorify you.

Help me to remember that no act of service is too small or insignificant when done in your name. Everything I do can glorify you. Show me how to live my entire life in keeping with your calling and your mission for me—your purpose for me.

Open my eyes to the opportunities you place before me and give me the wisdom to discern what you would have me do.

This I ask in Jesus' name.

Amen

Chapter 14: Abide in Me

The Meaning of "Abide"

Abide isn't a word we use too often these days, but it has a peaceful ring to it, don't you think? To "abide" means to "remain." In fact, the New International Version of the Holy Bible used throughout this book for scriptural references uses the word "remain" in the text rather than the word "abide." So to abide in Jesus means to remain in Jesus or to remain with Jesus at all times.

The beautiful scripture that calls us to abide or remain with Jesus in the 15th chapter in the book of John uses the story of the vine and the branches to show us that without Jesus, we can't do anything.

With Him, we can "go forth and bear fruit"—we can accomplish something worthwhile with our lives.

Without Him, we can do nothing.

If we are not spending daily time with Jesus, is it any wonder our lives feel empty—like something is missing? It feels like something is missing, because the most important part of our lives *is* missing!

We need Jesus in our life. We need His love, His guidance, His direction, and His peace. We need to honor His will for our lives to find fulfillment and joy. Without Him, it all feels meaningless...because it is.

How Do We Remain in Him?

To abide with Jesus, to remain in Him, is not as difficult as it sounds. Prayer is the easiest and most effective way to abide with Him. As you already know, to pray simply means to communicate with God—through words, song, meditation, and countless other ways.

When we abide in Jesus, we can "feel" His presence in our lives. We know He is with us always. He is an ever present help in our daily lives. We can go to Him any time, and we do. We spend time with Him throughout the day, every day. No day goes by that we don't think about Him and communicate with Him somehow, even if it is just to thank Him for a beautiful sunrise.

In fact, if we use the likeness of the branch and the vine that Jesus used to describe how we should abide in and remain with Him, we could even say that we are *attached* to Him as a branch is attached to a vine. We are always together, always a part of one another.

Jesus tells us that this is true. When he appeared to the eleven disciples in Galilee after His death and resurrection, he promised us: *"...I am with you always, to the very end of the age."* Matthew 28:20

We are never alone, but to abide with Jesus is to be conscious of His presence in our lives, to welcome that presence, and to enjoy and appreciate our relationship with Him.

Immerse Yourself in His Word

In addition to praying, you can develop a closer relationship with God by getting to know Him better. Reading His Word in the Holy Bible can give you insight into God's plan for your life and His ultimate plan for all of us. You can learn about God and gain wisdom from His Word.

Commit scriptures that are particularly meaningful to you to memory to sustain you through difficult days and help you celebrate your blessings with praise and thanksgiving.

Visit your church regularly and talk with your spiritual advisors who can help you learn even more about God and faith. Church attendance can help replenish your soul, make you feel closer to God, and refresh your spirit. Visiting God in His house, hearing the word of God, and listening to the sermon can greatly enhance your knowledge of God and thus your relationship with Him. Sharing fellowship and friendship with other believers is an opportunity for you to celebrate the joy and love you feel in the Lord with others who understand you.

Abiding in Him means that we do not separate our "daily life" from an hour each weekend when we do "the church thing." Abiding in Him means that our love for the Lord is intertwined with every part of our lives. The very fact that we are Christians should be evident in our daily existence and how we conduct ourselves. The love and peace that Jesus Christ brings to our lives should surround us every day and extend to our interactions with others.

Parallels With Other Experiences

In order to help you understand the concept of abiding, let me help you put it into perspective with some of our earthly experiences. You will soon come to know and recognize this feeling of abiding with Him for yourself as you develop a close and intimate relationship with Him.

When my children were babies, I remember rocking them in the quiet evening hours as they slept, my chin resting gently on the tops of their soft, downy heads. It was a peaceful, blissful moment when all seemed right with the world. I was happy and blessed, and it didn't matter that I wasn't saying anything. I didn't need to sing or hum or talk to the baby. We just were. Together, that baby and I shared something deep and meaningful that words could not express. We were surrounded by love.

This inexplicable feeling is what it is like to abide with God. Prayers may come to your mind, but words do not need to be spoken aloud. God knows your thoughts, and He knows your heart. You can feel His presence in your life even though you cannot physically see Him standing before you. You can close your eyes and feel the soft touch of His loving arms wrapped around you.

***

If you do not have children, think of a quiet Sunday morning waking up beside your husband. It is early and you can hear the birds outside your window. Soft light streams through your window and creates a hazy glow in the room. Your bed and pillow are soft, and your husband's arm is around you. You feel safe, secure, and content. Love surrounds and envelopes you in the stillness, though no words are spoken. You are relaxed and unhurried, enjoying the moment for what it is. A moment of peace.

***

Or perhaps you are lying on a blanket in the sun, warm and content. You are all alone on a beautiful summer day. There is just a hint of a breeze brushing against your skin. Overhead the trees rustle quietly, whispering to one another. Nearby, you can hear the roar of the ocean or the rushing of a stream. You are soaking up every moment of this quiet solitude. You are still, studying your surroundings and focusing on their beauty knowing that for this moment, all is right with your world. You are reflecting on happy days in your life and feeling totally at peace. All feels right with your world.

***

Abiding in Jesus can be compared to all of these experiences and so much more.

Abiding in Jesus is knowing that He is with you always and consciously taking the time to be with Him. It is basking in His very presence. It is fully feeling the peace and joy only He can give you. You can abide in the Lord at home or in church, in a park or in the supermarket, wherever you are and whatever you are doing. It is knowing that He is a part of your life—every day and in every way. It is walking with God daily and feeling secure in His love for you.

It requires no special skills and no special setting. It is all about *being with* Him. It is not about doing, but about being.

With Jesus By Your Side

With Jesus by your side, there is no limit to what you can do. God gives you the power to achieve what He has planned for you. When you abide in Him, you tap into that limitless power. Miracles can happen!

Your life will become richer and fuller than you ever imagined. Peace, love, and contentment will fill your soul, regardless of the circumstances that exist in the outside world.

"...I have come that they may have life, and have it to the full." John 10:10

- ✞ Do you take regular time each day to reflect on your spiritual life?
- ✞ Do you feel close to God?
- ✞ Where can you "escape" to spend time alone with God?
- ✞ How can you eliminate those things in your life that separate you from God?
- ✞ Do you feel the Lord's loving presence in your life?

Pray With Me...

Dear Lord,
There is no better place in this world to be than with you. When I am in your presence, everything seems to fall into place. I trust in you and your plan for my life. I am at peace and I feel content. Help me to increase the moments in my day when I truly abide with you, consciously experiencing your loving presence.

Guide me to eliminate those things that would distract me from increasing my time with you and sharing my life with you.

Show me how to extend the spirit of your love into all areas of my life and to share your love with others. Make my life a living testimony to your love as I walk with you and abide in you every moment of every day.

Amen

Chapter 15:
The Miracles

What is a Miracle?

Most of us think of physical healing when we hear the word "miracle." And Jesus did perform miracles of healing in His time here on earth, even bringing some people back to life after they had died. God still performs such miracles—healing people who are afflicted with diseases and conditions that defy human explanation. And even today we see people brought to life again after they technically died—through mouth-to-mouth resuscitation and other means that are certainly God's tools to perform such miracles.

He performed other miracles that defy physical explanation, as well—like feeding thousands of people with just a few fish and loaves of bread and then having more leftovers at the end of the meal than what he started out with at the beginning—and turning water into wine.

Jesus worked other miracles that we don't readily identify as miracles, too. Think about the apostles before they met Jesus and became His followers. They were everyday men of no special background—not kings or prophets. And some were despised as the lowlife of society—tax collectors and murderers.

God performed a miracle when He changed their hearts and enlisted them in His service. In fact, at least one of the apostles persecuted Christians before He came to know Jesus and Jesus miraculously changed his heart.

God continues to work such miracles in the hearts and minds of people all over this earth when He brings them into His kingdom through His gift of forgiveness.

Look For the Miracles

Miracles can occur in the physical realm, the spiritual realm, and in the heart and soul. God, with His almighty and limitless power, can perform miracles in any and all circumstances.

These days, it may simply be that many people deny the miracles in their lives. We need to open our eyes and *look* for the miracles! You will find an abundance of evidence to substantiate the existence of miracles if you want to find it. Similarly, there are people who deny the existence of God and will find every reason they can to refute the possibility of a miracle in their lives.

What will you choose to believe?

Subtle Miracles in Your Life

When you begin to pray and develop a special, ongoing, intimate relationship with God, you will be amazed at the miracles you begin to see in your life. Through your faith, you will experience miracles of many kinds.

You may see miraculous changes in the lives of the people you pray for—family and friends experiencing blessings they never imagined. Perhaps it will come in the form of healing, safety, good jobs, better marriages, children, or good homes.

You may also begin to see changes in outlook, attitude, cooperation, helpfulness, and behavior.

You will undoubtedly see miraculous changes in yourself. You will feel less uncertain and more confident—because you will no longer rely exclusively on yourself. You will be in partnership with God, and you will be tapping into His limitless power.

You will find an inner peace and comfort in knowing God that you cannot find from any other source. Regardless of the outside circumstances that affect you, your inner harmony with God will create a sanctuary of sorts that you can retreat to—a place where you know that together you and God will prevail and that He will use all circumstances to generate some good, even if you don't know what it is right away.

Your self-esteem will increase immeasurably because you know that you are loved without limits and that you were created just as you are with a very special purpose. You are a valuable person and God does not want you to be like someone else. You are unique, and He knows you and everything about you, and still He loves you more than anyone else ever will or ever can.

You can release your worries and troubles to God and know that never again will you struggle with them alone. In fact, if you give them over entirely to God, you can experience a tranquility you have never experienced before, even in the midst of a storm. Like an eagle, you can soar above the storm in grace and with ease—all because you trust in God.

You will have the assurance of blessings in your life and eternal salvation in heaven because God gave His one and only Son, Jesus, just for you!

Yes, through prayer, your life will undergo miraculous changes.

When you develop a special, intimate relationship with God, you are no longer alone. You will never again need to feel lost and alone and afraid. That feeling of emptiness will pass away because that "something missing" has been found. With

God, you are complete. You are whole. And you are free to live a blessed and prosperous life of abundance, enjoying all of the gifts and love He wants to give you because you are His precious, precious child, and this is your inheritance.

May you be blessed beyond your wildest dreams!

But the fruit of the Spirit is love, joy, peace, patience, kindness, goodness, faithfulness, gentleness and self-control. Galatians 5:22-23

Let us not become weary in doing good, for at the proper time we will reap a harvest if we do not give up. Galatians 6:9

"...No eye has seen, no ear has heard, no mind has conceived what God has prepared for those who love him." 1 Corinthians 2:9

When you call upon God's divine intervention for yourself and especially for others, God can provide for the seemingly impossible. Because with Him, all things really *are* possible.

Lives will be touched and souls will be saved by your prayers.

☦ Do you believe in miracles?
☦ How would you personally define a miracle?
☦ Do you believe in God's healing power—for illness, relationships, ill feelings, or *anything*?
☦ Do you trust God enough to ask Him for a miracle in your life?
☦ Do you want to change your life?
☦ Are you willing to let God go to work in your heart?

Pray With Me...

Dear Lord,
When I open my eyes to see the possibilities, I realize that miracles happen every day. I just have to be aware and alert to the fact that they exist and seek them in my life.

Never again will I feel powerless in the face of circumstances because I have faith in you. And though it may at times be a very small faith—yes, even as tiny as a mustard seed—it is faith. You promised that if I had faith in you, you could work miracles.

Sometimes what I pray for isn't in keeping with your greater plan. I can accept that, even if it is difficult to do so. But at other times, I know that you are simply waiting for me to come to you and trust you and ask for that miracle you want so much to give me. I will ask for that miracle, Lord.

And I ask for a miracle right now—for your love to perform a miraculous change in my heart and my soul and my spirit. I want to become closer to you and to find the peace, contentment, joy, and fulfillment that only you can bring to my life.

This I ask in the loving name of your beloved Son who gave His very life for me and my salvation, Jesus Christ.
Amen

Chapter 16:
The Journey

As you've read this book, you have taken the first tentative steps to developing a personal, intimate relationship with God. Perhaps you have even prayed fervently for God's intervention in your life in some way.

This is the beginning—the beginning of an eternal, loving relationship with a God you are just beginning to get to know. I promise you this is *the most important journey* you will *ever* embark on. You will never be disappointed you if you keep your heart open to doing His will and seeing His hand at work in your life.

Though it may sometimes be difficult, trust Him. Put your faith in Him and let it work. Sow the seed and just see what you will reap in the years to come.

Know and believe in your heart that God loves you no matter what you have done in the past or what your life has been like. He can forgive you *anything* and He does.

Know also that changes do not always come overnight. It may take time for you to find this peace and develop a comfortable rapport with God. That's OK. Just don't give up. Don't turn away from Him.

You don't have to be perfect and you don't have to say all the right things to get through to God. He comes to you where you are right now and welcomes you with open arms. He wants you to get to know Him and to ask Him into your life.

You don't need to be sophisticated or happy or perfect to be deserving of His love and compassion. In fact, God is a best friend to the poor and lonely, the depressed and troubled, and all of us who struggle to find a better way. He will show you the way if you will follow Him.

Jesus answered, "I am the way and the truth and the life. No one comes to the Father except through me." John 14:6

"For God so loved the world that he gave his one and only Son, that whoever believes in him shall not perish but have eternal life." John 3:16

A Journey, Not a Destination

Growing spiritually and developing a close, intimate relationship with God is a journey, not a destination. Beginning to pray and coming to know God is a part of the journey. No matter where you are in the process, it is never too late and you can never pray too much. We are all on this very same journey.

Your and my final destination is eternal life with Him in heaven, but even then we will continue to grow with Him.

Today the journey begins. Open your heart to Jesus. Miracles can happen when a woman prays... Miracles can happen when *you* pray.

If you are having trouble getting started, let me pray with you. Email me at: tina@tinalmiller.com. I will personally pray with you.

May God bless you richly and abundantly and beyond your wildest dreams!

- ✝ Do you have even a grain of faith to start with?
- ✝ Can you pray for more faith and trust in Him?
- ✝ Will you talk with Him and ask Him to help you grow?
- ✝ Do you want a close, intimate relationship with God?
- ✝ Are you willing to keep trying even when the going gets tough and never give up, if He promises never to give up on you?
- ✝ What are you waiting for?

My Prayer For You...

Dear Lord,
Through your divine intervention, this book came to be placed in this woman's hands. While my words may be inadequate to do you justice, I pray that you will place your Holy Spirit in the life of this woman and guide her to a close and loving relationship with you.

Enlighten her, give her wisdom, touch her heart. Stand by her side, wrap your loving arms around her, and help her to know the blessing of your unconditional love and forgiveness.

When she feels fragile, make her strong. When she feels inadequate, give her your reassurance that she can fulfill the mission you have in mind for her. When she doubts, grant her faith. When she is sad, fill her heart with your joy. When she is worried and fearful, grant her your peace. When she is hurting, hold her close to you until the pain subsides. When she is happy, rejoice with her in her blessings. Grant her your loving grace and mercy. Come into her life today and make her whole.

Amen

Share Your Stories

Miracles can happen when a woman prays. Prayers will be answered. Dreams will be fulfilled. Callings will be discovered. Faith will be restored. Forgiveness will be extended and accepted. Lives will be changed.

When you begin to pray every day and develop your own close, personal relationship with God, your life will change. Without a doubt, you will experience some remarkable discoveries in your life!

I'd like to hear about the changes in your life. Share your stories with me. In the future, we may even compile them into a book to share with others who are searching for meaning and fulfillment in their life—people who need to hear firsthand that God and prayer are what are missing in their lives. Maybe your story will make an eternal difference for someone...

You can send your true, personal stories via regular mail or email.

Snail mail:
        Tina L. Miller
        607 N. Cleveland Street
        Merrill, WI 54452

Email: tina@tinalmiller.com

Resources

Prayers

For those of you who don't know quite where to begin or how to start that dialogue with God, I thought I'd share a few impromptu prayers of my own. Feel free to use these prayers as they are or tweak them to fit your circumstances.

Soon you'll be so comfortable talking daily with God that you won't need my prayers at all!

Blessings to you!

A Prayer for Today

Dear God,
Thank you so much for today—a new beginning that lets me start over to try to do my best for you. You know all of the things I have planned today, Lord. I pray that you will help me accomplish them according to your will and that if there is something else more important you would want me to do instead, that you will show me what it is and guide me to do it so that it will be pleasing to you.

Guide my thoughts, words, and action and help me to be a witness to your love and your presence in my life to everyone I come into contact with today. Bless me and my family, keep us safe, and protect us as we go about our day.
Amen

A Prayer When You Feel Overwhelmed

Dear Lord,
Please give me strength right now. I feel so overwhelmed with everything—bills, kids, the job, and my endless list of things to do. It seems I will never get it all done. And the truth is, I probably won't. Help me to prioritize my time to accomplish those things *you* think I should accomplish. Give me the grace to let go of the things that really do not need to be done and are not a part of your plan for me. Give me the strength to do those things you want me to do.

Take away my worry and frustration and restore my soul with your peace and understanding. Fill my heart with joy knowing that you are here in my life with me, and I remind me that I am never alone. Guide me to do your will, oh, God.
Amen

A Prayer When You Are Scared or Worried

Dear God,
I am frightened. I am praying, and I know that you have things all under control, but right now I feel lost. I don't know what your plan is, and I'm scared. Right now it feels like darkness is surrounding me. I feel alone and lonely, and I don't know what to do to make things better. Sometimes it even feels like despair is about to set in. The only thing that keeps me from totally falling apart is the knowledge that you are here with me even if I cannot see you and sometimes I cannot feel your presence. You promised that you would never leave me or forsake me, and that is holding me together. But it is a very precarious holding it together just now.

Please, please give me the strength and wisdom to get through this situation. Show me what to do. Tell me what to say. Help me to do the right thing. Help me to overcome this fear, worry, and pain. Restore confidence and joy in my life. Show me your blessings. Show me your way.
Amen

A Prayer of Thanksgiving

Dear Lord,
Thank you so much for all of your blessings! I look around me and everything feels right with the world. I could never have imagined I would be so blessed. And it's all because of you. I am thankful I prayed that your will be done, because I'd never have dared to pray for so much for myself. I would have limited myself with my prayers. But you know no limits. You have blessed me with overwhelming abundance!

Praise you, Lord! Today my soul rejoices because of your boundless love and generosity. Help to make me truly worthy of your love and to share that love with others around me today and every day.
Amen

A Prayer For Someone Who Is Hurting

Dear Lord,
(Insert name here) is hurting, and I don't know what to do to help. I hurt for him/her and wish I could make it better. Give me the wisdom to do or say the right things. Help me to share your love and compassion with him/her and to provide comfort.

Grant him/her your mercy and love and help them through this difficult time of sorrow/grief/pain/illness and bring him/her out of the shadows and back into your light.

This I ask in Jesus' name,
Amen

A Prayer For a Loved One Who is Struggling

Dear Lord,
Please bless this friend/child/husband of mine who is struggling right now. Make your love and compassion known to him/her and help him/her to seek your guidance and direction in his/her life. I know that if he/she puts his/her trust in you, everything will be OK no matter what happens.

Help me, too, to say and do the right things to be a real asset to our relationship and to be a help to him/her. Show me what to do and say to be a witness to him/her without further troubling him/her.
Amen

A Prayer When You Are Depressed

Dear Lord,
I am depressed. I don't even know why exactly. It just feels like everything is out of sorts. I don't know what I want or how to get it. I am just floundering. Give me some direction. Cheer my soul. Help me focus my energy. Lift my spirits. Cover me with your grace. Please show me what to do.
Amen

People Who Want to Pray With You

There are many prayer groups in existence—composed of people who want to pray for you and your needs. If you would like someone to pray with or for you, feel free to contact any of these resources to share your prayer request.

"*Again, I tell you that if two of you on earth agree about anything you ask for, it will be done for you by my Father in heaven. For where two or three come together in my name, there am I with them.*" Matthew 17:19-20

Guideposts Prayer Fellowship
PO Box 8000
Pawling, NY 12564-8000
www.guideposts.com
&
Peale Center for Christian Living
The Outreach Division of Guideposts
PO Box 8001
Pawling, NY 12564
(914) 855-5000
www.guideposts.org
http://spiritual.crosswalk.com/prayer

700 Club
www.700club.com
24-hour prayer line: 1-800-759-0700

PrayerWeb
www.prayerweb.com

Prayer Ministry
www.prayer-ministry.com

eprayer
www.eprayer.org

World Ministry of Prayer
http://www.wmop.org

US Prayer Center
www.usprayercenter.org

America's National Prayer Committee
www.gospelcom.net/npc/index2.html

Family Life
www.familylife.com

You can find many, many sites where prayer requests are accepted on the Internet. While I have provided a few for you here, it's common for urls to change quickly. For the most current email addresses and urls, go to a search engine like www.google.com and do a search on the words "prayer request" to find links to web sites dealing with prayer and online forms that will allow you to post your prayer request directly.

If you would like to join a more personal group of people who regularly pray for each other's needs, you can subscribe to one of the following listservs at www.yahoogroups.com:
MomPrayers@yahoogroups.com
(Christian Moms praying for each other) or ObadiahPress@yahoogroups.com.

To join, send a blank email to either MomPrayers-subscribe@yahoogroups.com or ObadiahPress-subscribe@yahoogroups.com.

More Books About Prayer

To read more about prayer, positive thinking, and your gifts from God, check out these books:

The Prayer of Jabez by Bruce Wilkinson

Secrets of the Vine by Bruce Wilkinson

The Power of a Praying Wife by Stormie O'Martian

The Power of Positive Thinking by Norman Vincent Peale

Reaching Your Potential by Norman Vincent Peale

Bible Power for Successful Living by Norman Vincent Peale

The Positive Power of Jesus Christ by Norman Vincent Peale

Stay Alive All Your Life by Norman Vincent Peale

Discovering the Power of Positive Thinking by Norman Vincent Peale and Ruth Stafford Peale

The Amazing Results of Positive Thinking by Norman Vincent Peale

God is my CEO by Larry Julian

Let Prayer Change Your Life by Becky Tirabassi

The Complete Idiot's Guide to Prayer by Mark Galli and James S. Bell Jr.

Prayer Can Change Your Life by Dr. William R. Parker and Elaine St. Johns

Power Thoughts by Robert Schuller

If It's Going to Be, It's up to Me by Robert Schuller

The Call of a Lifetime by Michael Youssef

Gifts of the Spirit by Kenneth Cain Kinghorn

The Holy Bible

About the Author

Tina L. Miller is a freelance writer and motivational speaker with a personal mission: to motivate and inspire others.
  She enjoys writing about people and relationships, self-help and improvement, families, parenting, the writing life, health and wellness, management, leadership, and business and entrepreneurial issues. In addition, she is a prolific writer who writes for newspapers and magazines, the web, businesses, and corporations. Her work has appeared in print and online publications including: the *Wausau Daily Herald, Milwaukee Business Journal, Merrill Courier, COBRA Advisory, The Writing Parent, Inklings, Spare Time, Wines & Vines, Secrets & Strategies of the Office Professional, Obadiah Magazine,* AllBusiness.com, FitnessHeaven.com, Herdlinger.com, FamilyClick.com, Showbix.com, and many others.
  She has written and presents such programs as *"Discovering Your God-Given Gifts," "Dare to Live Your Dreams,"* and *"Discovering the Power of Prayer."*
  She also does editing/layout for other authors and is the Editor in Chief of *Obadiah Magazine.*
  Tina lives in Merrill, Wisconsin, with her husband, John, and two children.

http://www.tinalmiller.com
email: tina@tinalmiller.com.

Order Other Books Published by:

OBADIAH PRESS

Qty. Ordered

___Running As Fast As I Can@ $16.95
by Lois Hilton Spoon
Exactly one year from the day she was told she would die from terminal cancer, Lois ran a ten mile race, and she hasn't slowed down since. A story of hope, God's miraculous intervention, and life, the stories from this book will fly from the pages into your heart.

___Good Mourning, Lord@ $15.95
by Alyice Edrich
When her child died, a part of Alyice did, too. Raw and emotionally poignant, she shares her feelings and provides room for you to journal your own feelings as you work through *your* grief, knowing there is no "right way" to grieve.

___More Coffee, God?@ $10.95
by Sallie Bachar
Start your day reflecting on God's word and His influence in your life.

___Good Morning Lord Jesus!@$14.95
by Martha Langley
A quiet time praise and prayer book for children.

___How to Write for Websites, Ezines, and Newsletters@ $14.95   *by Kyle Looby*
A guide to freelance writing online: finding markets and jobs, writing a killer query, getting ideas, researching, negotiating contracts, and more! Includes guidelines for *400 online paying markets!*

Total for books ordered above = $_____
___# of books ordered in total
    x $2 S/H per book = $_____

TOTAL ENCLOSED = $_____
(Make checks or MO payable to: **Obadiah Press**)

Send orders with payment to:
Obadiah Press
607 N. Cleveland Street
Merrill, WI 54452

Ship Books to:
Name_____
Address_____

Prices shown are US funds. Include $2 additional for Canadian orders and $4 additional for other international orders. Quantity discounts available. Write for information. This form may be freely reproduced.

OBADIAH PRESS
A Christian Publishing House

Order Form

Please send ____ copies of When A Woman Prays by Tina L. Miller to:

Name: _____

Address: _____

City: _____ State: _____

Zip: _____

Country: _____

Telephone: _____

Book Price: $15.95 in U.S. dollars

Shipping & Handling: $2.00 in U.S. dollars per book
(Include $2 additional for Canadian orders and $4 additional for other international orders.)

Make checks or money order payable to: Obadiah Press

Send orders with payment to: Obadiah Press
607 N. Cleveland Street
Merrill, WI 54452

Quantity discounts available. Write for information.
This form may be freely reproduced.

OBADIAH PRESS
A Christian Publishing House

Order Form

Please send ____ copies of When A Woman Prays by Tina L. Miller to:

Name: _____

Address: _____

City: _____ State: _____

Zip: _____

Country: _____

Telephone: _____

Book Price: $15.95 in U.S. dollars

Shipping & Handling: $2.00 in U.S. dollars per book (Include $2 additional for Canadian orders and $4 additional for other international orders.)

Make checks or money order payable to: Obadiah Press

Send orders with payment to: **Obadiah Press**
607 N. Cleveland Street
Merrill, WI 54452

Quantity discounts available. Write for information.
This form may be freely reproduced.

OBADIAH MAGAZINE

For People Who Live Their Lives to Love and Serve the Lord

Just $15 for 4 quarterly issues!
Canadian subscriptions: $18
Other International subscriptions: $20

Subscribe Me!

Mail To: Obadiah Magazine
c/o Obadiah Press
1826 Crossover Road, PMB 108
Fayetteville, AR 72703

Name: _____

Address: _____
_____

City, State, Zip: _____

Country: _____ Phone: _____

Include check or money order (US funds) for each subscription ordered.

Initial Subscription: _____ Renewal: _____ (check one)

Did anyone refer you to Obadiah Magazine? If so, please include their name here. They may be eligible to win a $100 prize in our "Most Subscription Referrals Contest."
_____

Send a Gift Subscription:

Mail To: Obadiah Magazine
c/o Obadiah Press
1826 Crossover Road, PMB 108
Fayetteville, AR 72703

Please send a gift subscription TO:

Name: _____

Address: _____
_____

City, State, Zip: _____

Country: _____ Phone: _____

FROM: _____

NOTE TO INCLUDE WITH FIRST ISSUE: _____
_____
_____

Include check or money order (US funds) for each subscription ordered.

This form may be freely reproduced.